D0680910

From start to finish

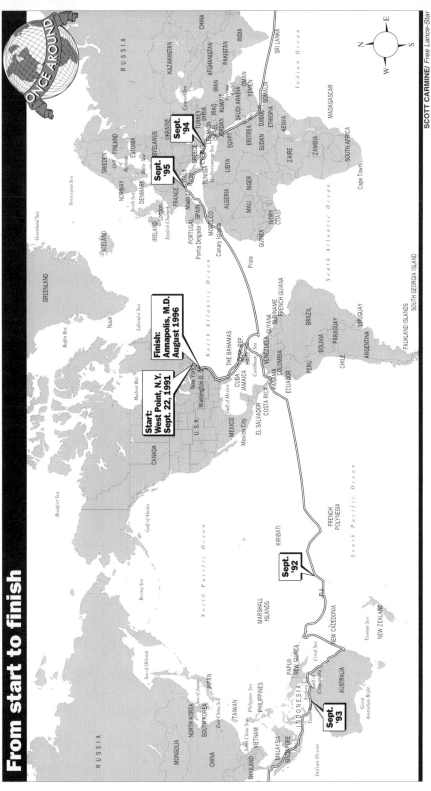

Start:
West Point, N.Y.
Sept. 22, 1991

Finish:
Annapolis, M.D.
August 1996

Sept. '92

Sept. '93

Sept. '94

Sept. '95

SCOTT CARMINE/ *Free Lance-Star*

ONCE AROUND

ONCE AROUND

Ward and Judy LeHardy

In a series of articles that first appeared in the Free Lance-Star of Fredericksburg, Virginia, this couple chronicles the fulfillment of a life-long dream; sailing around the world in their 39-foot boat, CORMORANT.

Library of Congress Catalog Card Number: 96-92991

First Edition - January, 1997
Second Edition - October, 1997

Cover Logo by Scott Carmine/Free Lance-Star

THIS BOOK IS DEDICATED TO THE MEN AND WOMEN OF THE ARMED FORCES OF THE UNITED STATES OF AMERICA WHO SERVED DURING THE "COLD WAR". THEIR ACHIEVEMENTS AND SACRIFICES DURING A PERIOD OF MORE THAN 40 YEARS HELPED TO DEFEAT THE SOVIET UNION, AND MADE A JOURNEY SUCH AS OURS POSSIBLE.

FOREWORD

As far back as we can remember we have talked of sailing around the world. We wanted to do it by ourselves, in our own boat, with friends and family joining us when they could.

We were both raised in Navy families, but spent thirty-two years of our married life in the Army after Ward graduated from West Point in 1956. No doubt a part of us yearned for the sea, and the freedom to roam the world over.

Our adventure began when we were in our mid-fifties. Fortunately, we were in good health and reasonably fit, for this trip would require more stamina and physical strength than we could have imagined. We had some knowledge of sailing, having owned two smaller sailboats, but we had never sailed on the ocean overnight. Two years after buying CORMORANT, we made a trial run to Bermuda, and three months later set off around the world.

We knew we would make mistakes along the way, and that we would learn from them. Being self-sufficient was the key to this entire journey.... doing the best we could with what we had.

Leaving our four grown children and four grandchildren was difficult, but we knew they would grow closer to each other as a result of our absence. Through various means of communications, our visits back home, and their times with us at sea, we managed to stay close to them. Three of our children met their future spouses and were married during our trip, and two more grandchildren came into our lives.

We learned to communicate better with each other, too. Living on a 39-foot sailboat, depending on each other for our very survival, brought us even closer than we had been during thirty-five years of marriage. We also learned to communicate with God, and remain in constant touch with Him.

As we revealed our plans to friends and family, many were incredulous. One of Ward's aunts asked, admonishingly: "Did your mother know you wanted to do this?" Others exclaimed: "Awesome!" "Unbelievable!" "You must be very brave or very stupid!". Most of our Navy friends, who had spent years at sea, thought we were crazy. Our Army friends, who had been landlocked on Army posts in Kentucky, Kansas, or Colorado, said: "Go for it!"

Ward's classmate, Dave Palmer, then Superintendent of the U.S. Military Academy, suggested that our departure be from West Point, New York following the 35th reunion of the Class of 1956. Our trip became a "Victory Lap", once around the world, celebrating the end of the "Cold War".

As that date approached, we discussed with the Free Lance-Star, the daily newspaper of Fredericksburg, Virginia, the idea of writing a monthly column to keep our hometown informed of our progress. Maria Carrillo was assigned as our editor and became our friend.

This book is a collection of those monthly articles, modified slightly to improve the flow. The articles, illustrations and photographs are printed here with permission of the Free Lance-Star.

CONTENTS

WEST POINT to PANAMA. . . . . .page 9

PANAMA to TAHITI. . . . . page 43

BORA BORA to AUSTRALIA. . . . . page 67

AUSTRALIA. . . . . .page 105

SOUTHEAST ASIA. . . . . .page 135

THAILAND to CYPRUS. . . . . .page 171

CYPRUS to ITALY. . . . . page 205

ITALY to MOROCCO. . . . . page 231

MOROCCO to ANNAPOLIS. . . . . .page 255

DESCRIPTION of CORMORANT. . . . . . . .page 287

AFTERWORD. . . . . .page 289

Leaving West Point: sailing down the Hudson River

WEST POINT TO PANAMA

"They that go down to the sea in ships,
that do business in great waters;
These see the works of the Lord,
and His wonders in the deep."

Psalm 107: 23-24.

WE SET SAIL ON A DREAM
(A rousing send-off: the adventure begins)

Pitch black....cold...wind blowing at 20 knots, breezing us along the Jersey Coast. Stars starting to pop out from the diminishing clouds. One by one they sparkle to life until the awesome power of God's universe blankets us overhead in a million white lights.

Almost simultaneously, two large, glowing red objects appear on the horizon; one to our front, the other behind us. Astern, it's the full moon still partially obscured by black clouds. Ahead, a red glob continues to emerge. A half-hour later it is obvious that Atlantic City is rising from the horizon, the red glow being the top of Donald Trump's Taj Mahal. Both the full moon and Atlantic City will stay with us through the night at sea. We prefer the glowing moon to the gamblers' mecca.

*   *   *   *   *

We had left West Point two days earlier, on September 22nd, 1991, for the "official" start of our five-year sail around the world. About one hundred and fifty people came to South Dock on the Hudson River to see us off, including good friends Norm and Brenda Schwarzkopf.

Three of our children, three of our grandchildren, and a host of other relatives, classmates and friends climbed all over our boat wanting to see where we would be living for the next four years. Many were dumbfounded at the relatively cramped area, while others, who had been around sailboats, were visibly impressed.

CORMORANT had been painstakingly built by Don Ney, the former owner, over three years. He created a spacious boat, ruggedly built to withstand ocean sailing yet appointed to make it feel like home.

After all the toasts, photographs and hoopla, the Reverend Harry Crandall, a West Point classmate, led us all in prayer. He asked God to watch over us and our boat and to provide us with the "wit and wisdom to overcome the challenges" that certainly lay ahead. He blessed the boat, and then the moment came for us to shove off.

Our daughter, Sally Kellogg, and her three children, Durrant, Sara, and James, cut the ribbon that linked us to a ferryboat full of friends. We had finally ended the years of planning and preparing, and were actually on our way. The end of one way of life and the start of another.

The crowded ferryboat followed us down the Hudson River for a mile or so. We wanted to look like a sailboat for them, so we raised all sails and began tacking back and forth down the narrow river. Our son Peter, a 1989 graduate of the U.S. Naval Academy, home on leave from San Diego, came with us on our first day. He had just returned from a six-month deployment to the Persian Gulf on the USS STEIN.

As the ferryboat tooted a final farewell and turned back toward West Point, we held up a large sign that read: "SO LONG '56, SEE YOU IN '96" (our next reunion). Our oldest son, Ward, Jr., a commercial video producer, captured the event on film.

Then, as if on cue, our first challenge arose. The engine overheated....it had been backing us up at a slow forward speed while we showed off our sails. We shut the engine off and now we HAD to sail. So we did, thirty miles downriver to the Tappan Zee Bridge and an anchorage in the lee of the New York Palisades. It took more than forty tacks to get there. We were glad to have Peter's help! That night we temporarily fixed the overheating engine and the next day motored the rest of the way down the Hudson.

*   *   *   *   *

11

Probably the best way to visit New York City is by boat. It appears clean and massive as you pass at five miles an hour. The George Washington Bridge, the Empire State Building, the Twin Towers at the Battery, Ellis Island, the Statue of Liberty and finally our destination, Governors Island. From the water you don't see the homeless, the crime and the poverty that are paralyzing parts of this gateway city.

*   *   *   *   *

A few days in Annapolis, Maryland after our trip from New York gave us time for some needed repairs. Annapolis is the sailing capital of the East Coast, and the best place to have work done. It took twelve hours of labor and a new saltwater pump to fix our overheating engine.

We left Annapolis in our wake with family and friends on the dock, including Judy's eighty-seven year old stepfather, Rear Admiral Joe Nevins. We had plenty of mixed emotions, wondering when or even if we'd see them again. Thank heavens God is in charge, and we continue to thank Him for our good fortune and fair winds.

SOUTHERN COMFORTS
(Hospitality in the Carolinas)

Dawn is breaking. Mist rises from the dark waters of the Alligator River. Off in the distance a dog barks. A hawk circles lazily. It is so still. No civilization is in sight except for five other sailboats laying at anchor nearby. The sun pops up over the pine trees on the far bank. It's the start of a clear and beautiful day in North Carolina.

*   *   *   *   *

After leaving Annapolis on October 10th and an overnight sail to Windmill Point at the mouth of the Rappahannock River, we continued on to Hampton, Virginia.

We tied up at Fort Monroe, a spot well worth visiting. The fort was built in 1819 to protect Hampton Roads. Deep in the heart of the massive stone fortress is the cell where Jefferson Davis was imprisoned after the Civil War. Edgar Allen Poe wrote poetry there and Army Lieutenant Robert E. Lee lived in quarters nearby in the 1830's. The Chamberlain Hotel at Fort Monroe, open to the public, overlooks Hampton Roads. From there President Lincoln watched the famous battle between the ironclads Monitor and Merrimac.

We crossed Hampton Roads on a fresh breeze, sailing past some of our Navy's current fleet of "ironclads." Lined up at the Norfolk Naval Base were aircraft carriers, submarines, and a host of supporting vessels.

In the heart of the Elizabeth River, at Norfolk's waterfront park, the renowned Intracoastal Waterway begins. It ends 1,095 miles further south in Miami. We continued down the narrowing and winding river and into the Dismal Swamp Canal. Digging for the canal started in 1793, and it opened for traffic in 1805. The canal is now maintained by the Army Corps of Engineers as the waterway between the Elizabeth and Pasquotank rivers.

We found the canal to be picturesque and anything but dismal. At Deep Creek Locks in Virginia, we picked up Dick Johns and his family to crew for us that day. Dick was the Army's Norfolk District Engineer, and a good friend. We were lifted up eight feet in those locks and twenty miles later we locked down at South Mills, North Carolina. Despite warnings from other sailors about shallow water in the canal, we found the depth averaged a comfortable nine feet. (CORMORANT draws about six feet when fully loaded.)

In North Carolina we stopped at the only visitor's center we know of that serves both boats and cars, along U.S. Route 17, which parallels the Canal. There we met director Penny Leary, who personifies southern hospitality.

A surprise lay ahead three hours away in Elizabeth City. Penny and Dick had passed the word that we were setting out on an around the world sail. The Mayor, Police Chief, and City Manager turned out to greet us when we pulled into the city docks. The City Attorney, Skip Hall, who had served with Ward in Korea thirty-four years before, was there as well. The local newspaper put us on the front page the next day!

In Elizabeth City boaters are greeted by the "Rose Buddies." For more than eight years, locals have been welcoming the ladies with a rose, and hosting a nightly wine and cheese party on the city docks. Boaters are given free docking for forty-eight hours at the Mariners' Wharf. Fred Fearing, the leader of the "Rose Buddies", is the proud recipient of a "Thousand Points of Light" certificate from President Bush for his work.

We stayed longer than we had planned, waiting for

better weather, and enjoyed meeting other boaters and townspeople. We were thankful to be at the dock rather than rounding Cape Hatteras or crossing Albemarle Sound, as gale force winds and rain whipped the area for two days.

Finally we were off, leaving new friends behind as we sailed and motored the remaining two days to Beaufort, North Carolina. Beaufort is a sailor's paradise, with ample dock space (though not free) and a wide, deep anchorage within one hour of the open ocean. Here we made minor repairs, changed the engine oil, and got ready to sail the ocean for two days and nights south to Charleston, South Carolina.

*   *   *   *   *

Along our course many people ask us why we're sailing around the world and how we can stand to leave our grandchildren for so long. We tell people we've been on a journey all our lives. During our thirty-five years of marriage we moved twenty-eight times with Ward's Army career. Home is wherever we happen to be.

We both believe that it is the journey of life, and not the destination, that is important. And we believe in that old saying, "You only go around once in life, so live it to the fullest."

SAILING SOUTH
(Nature and history give way to condos)

THUMP...THUMP...BUMP. Probably the most dreaded sounds to any skipper. It means you've hit bottom. Unfortunately that happens all too frequently on the Intracoastal Waterway. We hit bottom or ran aground five times during our trip down the ICW from Norfolk to Ft. Lauderdale.

Some of those bumps happened in the middle of the channel. As old-timers tell us, "If you haven't run aground, you haven't traveled the Waterway." None of our bumps or groundings lasted long. At the worst we were hung up for ten minutes until we could power our way to deeper water.

Leaving Beaufort, North Carolina (pronounced BOH-fort, while the historic city of the same spelling in South Carolina is pronounced BU-furt), we had an ocean stretch of forty-eight hours where we never changed the set of our sails. Whenever weather permitted, we chose the "outside" route, the sea, but if the wind came from the direction we wanted to go, we opted for the "inside" route.

By taking the Waterway, we were able to visit a few of the historic cities in the South. In Charleston we waited out a storm that roared up the East Coast in early November. It was in Charleston, at Fort Sumter, where the first shots of the Civil War were fired. Of course, here in the Deep South it's remembered as the War Between the States.

We took a "busman's holiday" and visited Fort Sumter by ferryboat. On this tiny island in the middle of Charleston Harbor Union forces withstood thirty-four hours of intense bombardment by Confederate artillery before withdrawing. The Confederate forces then occupied the fort and later in the war held it during more than seven-

16

teen months of Union shelling and attacks. The fort was turned to rubble but never surrendered.

Charleston boasts of its waterfront park, The Battery, and historic district, South of Broad Street. We stopped by St. Michael's Episcopal Church, built in 1761 and a survivor of wars, hurricanes and earthquakes. It is a great old church built on the spot where Christianity was first preached here in the 1680s.

*　　*　　*　　*　　*

A day's sail on the ocean and a few hours on the Waterway brought us to Savannah, Georgia, the home town of both of Ward's parents. Ward's cousin Luke Bowyer and his wife Johnny met us at their dock and cared for us and CORMORANT as we enjoyed a quiet weekend in this lacy, Spanish-mossed city. Here, the city squares have been preserved as parks and the riverfront completely restored; the aura of the Deep South fills the air.

We paid a visit to Bonaventure Cemetery, where many of Ward's family are buried, including the first LeHardy to arrive in America in the mid-1800's. As we motored south from Savannah we realized the Waterway passes directly below that plot of land. We spent a night at the dock of another of Ward's cousins, Tommie and Bev Leigh, before heading south. Savannah was bitter cold the entire weekend; we were still searching for warm weather.

Travelling the Waterway at night is risky. It is shallow and narrow, and has too many twists and turns to navigate after dark with confidence. We anchored each night we were in Georgia, and on one night fought off the chill with a wood fire in our on board fireplace.

Another day on the ocean brought us to St. Augustine, Florida. It was a dicey entry from the sea, across shifting sandbars with waves breaking on both sides and a stiff breeze pushing us. We anchored in the lee of the old Spanish fort, Castillo de San Marcos and met with an old friend, Dick Tripp, who had been in our wedding. Dick showed us the sights and we quickly appreciated the charming blend of Spanish and Southern cultures and customs. Here Ponce de Leon found his Fountain of Youth, and a building said to be the oldest structure in the country still stands.

While there are pockets of real beauty, opulence, and lush growth south of St. Augustine, a certain sameness prevails. Too many condos, too many people, and too many boats. But at last we found warm weather.

We anchored overnight at Singer Island, for a visit with Judy's eighty-six year old aunt, Ruth Anderson, and her friend, Peg Turner. Ruth came on board COR-MORANT in New Jersey before we left, and is one of our most enthusiastic supporters.

Florida's Waterway, especially as you approach Fort Lauderdale, is strangely devoid of wildlife. We had become accustomed to porpoises plunging along beside us in the inlets and creeks of South Carolina and Georgia. For many miles of our Waterway travel we were absorbed watching pelicans dive bombing for their lunch. All the way from New York to Florida the sleek cormorants, our boat's namesakes, entertained us with their speed and versatility. But in the waterways of Fort Lauderdale, people and activity seemed to have driven them away.

*   *   *   *   *

Communication is critical to what we're doing, not only between ourselves but with others. We have been blessed by being part of a network of Ham Radio operators, headed by Fred Chapman. We met Fred and his wife, Bonnie, at Church of the Messiah in Fredericksburg.

Fred coordinates the Afloat Net, part of the Navy-

Marine Corps MARS system. The Afloat Net was to be our radio link with the rest of the world. For us, meeting Fred was a match made in heaven. We looked forward to being "patched through" from radio to telephone by Fred and the many other volunteers on the Net as we left the mainland behind.

OFFSHORE AT LAST
(We cross the Gulf Stream, aim for the Virgin Islands)

Dead ahead lies the Gulf Stream. This massive river in the ocean is thirty miles wide, and we're about to cross it. The current would push us northward at 3 knots, so we adjust our direction southward in order to land at Bimini. It's a sparkling day, with a fresh 15-knot breeze. We estimate landfall in ten hours.

Five hours after leaving Ft. Lauderdale, we no longer see the Florida coast nor do we see our island destination. Only huge porpoises frolicking beside us, and an occasional boat or plane disturbs the moment. Even though it's a clear day, we turn on our radar, which reaches out twenty-four miles. BINGO! The bright green screen shows the Florida coast receding off our stern, and to our left front the flicker of an island...Bimini, twenty miles away.

*   *   *   *   *

We had spent almost three weeks at Ft. Lauderdale, most of the time seeking solutions to some enormous mechanical problems. One end of the engine oil cooler had disintegrated in Ward's hands as he removed it for cleaning. Calls to dealers in New Jersey and California indicated it would be four months before a replacement part could be shipped from the manufacturer in Germany. Undaunted, we found a machine shop that built the part for a fraction of the cost of a new one.

The stopover in Ft. Lauderdale allowed us to have Thanksgiving dinner with Charlie and Pat Poole, who took us under their wing for two weeks. We attended the huge Coral Ridge Presbyterian Church and also the First Presbyterian Church. Each was awesome, in its

20

own way. We also stocked up on parts, charts, food, fuel, and water for our departure from the U.S.

*　　*　　*　　*　　*

Bimini! The name conjures up thoughts of Ernest Hemingway, and more recently the tryst of Gary Hart and Donna Rice, which probably cost him a chance to be President.

We threaded our way into the harbor, cleared in with Customs at our first foreign port, anchored in the crystal clear waters, and rowed ashore. Winter is a dull time in Bimini! Alice Town, while quaint and rustic, was not a lively place. The Compleat Angler, the "watering hole" where Hemingway and Hart hung out, was quiet; not the bustling, rambunctious place we thought it would be.

We sailed the next day for Nassau, the capital of the Bahamas, two days away. Calm seas and light winds caused us to motor most of the way. As we entered Nassau Harbor we had to squeeze past four cruise ships, and then found a wonderful anchorage just off "Elkin's dock". Elkin is a friendly twelve year old boy who lives with his family on a listing, old trawler. For a dollar Elkin guarded our dinghy whenever we rowed ashore.

Weather normally reaches Nassau about twelve hours after it passes Ft. Lauderdale. Through our radio contacts in Florida, Ken Hookansen and Vince Roebuck, we learned of the cold front that was about to hit us. With two anchors down, we were able to hold our ground in the 40-knot winds and four foot seas that swept through Nassau Harbor the next day. During that time two of our sons, Ward and Peter, arrived by plane. This marked the first time any of our children came home to a boat for Christmas!

Finally the weather eased sufficiently for us to head out of Nassau, bound for Georgetown, Great Exuma, a three day sail away. Stops at the Exuma Cays Land and Sea Park on Warderick Wells Cay and Little Farmers Cay broke the trip up nicely. At each stop the clarity of the water and its variety of hues of blue astounded us.

In these magical isles we met some fascinating people, one of whom was the Park Ranger of the Exuma Cays Land and Sea Park, Peggy Hall. Peggy is a salty seventy year old who rules the nature park of some two hundred square miles by radio and high powered speed boat. She lives alone aboard her miniature tug boat, MOBY, with her faithful dog, Powerful. Peggy leaves at the crack of dawn each day to patrol the waters of the park looking for poachers.

Georgetown is the sailing capital of the Exumas and at Christmas we found well over two hundred boats anchored there. Among them was AT EASE, home to our friends of forty years, Jerry and Nancy Amlong from Baltimore. Three months earlier we had said we might meet in Georgetown for Christmas and, overcoming many obstacles, we did. We shared a turkey on their boat as the sun set at the end of a perfect Christmas day.

We ended our week together with our sons by attending the annual "Junkanoo" festival. At 3:00 a.m. on the twenty-sixth of December, the people of Georgetown turn out en masse in colorful costumes to chant and sway to a rhythmic beat for over five hours. Quite a spectacle, which left us all exhausted just watching it.

*   *   *   *   *

The day before Christmas we learned by radio that Judy's stepfather had died after a sudden illness. This was our first serious emotional dilemma since beginning our trip in September. We reflected on the many memorable moments we'd had with him, the last being our departure from Annapolis in October. Our last sight of him was his very positive "thumbs up" as we sailed away. We elected not to interrupt our trip to return for the funeral, and we are convinced that he would have wanted it that way.

After Ward and Peter departed, we headed offshore towards the Virgin Islands, our first lengthy ocean passage alone. We would celebrate New Year's Eve somewhere on the high seas!

Ward and Peter in the Bahamas

A PERSONAL REVELATION
(We find divine guidance in a storm)

Sailing reminds Ward of combat in Vietnam. Ninety-nine percent is absolutely routine; one per cent is sheer terror.

That roughly describes our trip from the Bahamas to the Virgin Islands, a distance of eight hundred miles out of sight of land. We had six days of pleasant, uneventful sailing, and four days of storms in which there were about three harrowing minutes.

We have had experience in heavy weather sailing and don't dread it, for we know our boat is sturdy. We have learned to be prepared for bad weather in advance, and reef the sails early. With just the two of us on board, we double-reef the mainsail every night, no matter what the weather prediction.

We also know that God is in charge, and we trust Him for our protection. What we learned on the way to the Virgin Islands is that God will also use circumstances to teach.

*   *   *   *   *

San Salvador was our last landfall in the Bahamas, and we enjoyed touring the island in the back of a pickup truck with some friendly Brits and Americans. We walked where Columbus first set foot in the "New World", and visited the Anglican church in downtown Cockburn Town. After thirty-six hours at anchor we set sail, bristling with confidence as we faced our first open-ocean passage to the Virgin Islands.

New Year's Eve was celebrated with a kiss as we swapped off the watch at midnight, three hundred miles from the nearest land. As the New Year dawned, two days out of San Salvador, signs of pending bad weather started to appear. The clouds were building, the seas were getting rougher, intermittent rain showers doused us, and the wind gusted to 25 knots.

After three days and nights of this stormy weather, we got used to a double-reefed mainsail, and the wet, rolling, nasty conditions. We lived in our yellow foul weather gear, often too exhausted to remove it when off watch. Below in the cabin it was dry, but we both preferred to be topside in the fresh, wet, tropical air. Through it all Judy kept producing hot meals, at least once a day.

At midnight on our fourth stormy night, the radar screen showed the biggest storm we had seen yet. It blotted out the entire screen, so we knew we'd be in it for many hours. We decided to "heave to" (set the sails so they counteract each other, producing no forward movement, while pointing the boat into the wind). At 2:00 a.m. we were both below watching the radar screen from the protection of the cabin, while the wind howled outside and the seas rushed by with tremendous force.

Suddenly, wind gusts of over 40 knots pushed COR-MORANT on her side, and water started pouring down one of the air vents we had forgotten to close. It was as if someone were pointing a fire hose full blast into the cabin.

Judy quickly grabbed a bucket to start bailing, as Ward leaped to the cockpit, where he saw the end of the boom dip into the oncoming rush of water. He quickly released the lines securing the sails, and the boat immediately righted itself. We then rushed to start the motor as a backup for the sails while we sorted out the messy situation. Hearts in our throats, we asked for God's help......the motor started instantly! The bilge pump engaged and the water in the cabin was pumped overboard within minutes. We went back to normality...wet, rolly, pitch black...with our cabin in a shambles, but the crisis was over.

*　　*　　*　　*　　*

Dawn found us still double-reefed, as yet another squall approached. Ward was at the helm; Judy asleep down below in her foul weather gear, exhausted.

Ward asked God for guidance on how best to avoid this new storm, and to his astonishment, a voice seemed to say, "Don't avoid it, go into it!" So CORMORANT headed into the storm. An incredible surge of confidence came over Ward, and he actually carried on a one-hour conversation with "someone". That voice gave him tips, directions on sails, and crystal-clear guidance on other questions he had been pondering.

It was a time of revelation, and ended when Ward announced he'd had enough schooling for one day! The voice told him, "O.K., head off to the west, there you'll find clear skies." Within a half-hour we were clear of the squall and the sun started to emerge.

Later, as we reviewed our actions during the terrifying moments of the five day storm, we both said the same thing: we were really not frightened, we were calm in taking swift action, and we each felt a strong reassuring presence of a third person on board. We both received guidance on what actions to take, and we both had a strange sense that the shore was nearby, even though we were over three hundred miles from land.

We reached St. Thomas on our tenth day out of San Salvador. The journey should have taken six or seven days, but the stormy weather, along with an unexpected south wind, rather than the prevailing east wind, caused the delay. As the memories of the five rough days faded, the lessons remained:

* Sometimes you need to face the storms of life head-on.
* If you trust in God, He will be with you, always.

* Be calm and confident in a crisis, even if you're not!
* Plan for the worst, then you'll be prepared for any eventuality.
* Check and double-check your preparations.
* If you ask God for help, be listening for an answer.

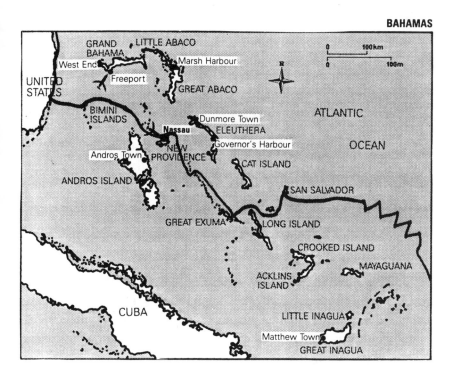

SAILING THE VIRGIN ISLANDS
("Painkillers" and a donkey named Vanilla)

Our ten difficult days at sea were soon followed by ten glorious days sailing in the Virgin Islands with our old friends John and Sara Wells, who had flown in from Coronado, California.

We swam, snorkeled, picnicked on beautiful sandy beaches, and hiked nature trails after each leisurely day of sailing from one sunny island to the next. We ate fresh caught lobster and drank the favorite local rum drink, "Pusser's Painkillers" at Sydney's Peace and Love native restaurant on Jost Van Dyke Island.

At one anchorage, Francis Bay on St. John, we saw the replicas of Columbus' three ships: the NINA, the PINTA, and the SANTA MARIA glide in and anchor along with us and the twenty other sailboats there! The next day we watched as helicopters and small power boats hovered near by, filming them as they "landed" ashore, marking the 500th anniversary of Columbus' discovery of America.

*   *   *   *   *

As we put the Wells on their plane in St. Croix, we met other friends, Chuck and Elaine Hood. Chuck is The Adjutant General (Senior National Guard officer) in the US Virgin Islands. The Hoods took us to Sunday services at their church, cooled by sea breezes, then showed us the sights of this the largest of the US Virgin Islands, where Hurricane Hugo wrought such devastation in 1989.

We visited the only site on what is now U.S.-owned land where Columbus landed...Salt River. In fact, only his initial landing party came ashore, quickly withdrawing to their ships when attacked by natives. Columbus decided not to go ashore, and departed for friendlier islands.

We needed time for repairs, and raced the sixty-two miles to Puerto Rico in ten hours. We spent two weeks at the Roosevelt Roads Marina, where the prices were right. There we removed varnish (an indication that we were really becoming ocean-going sailors, giving up the "yachty look"), installed parts, made minor repairs, and stocked up on provisions. One day we went into bustling San Juan to see Raphael LeHardy, a distant cousin of Ward's whom we had never met.

A two-day sail, with overnight anchorage at the island of Culebra, brought us back to St. Thomas. There we met up again with the Amlongs on AT EASE. They were slowly making their way to Venezuela, always waiting for favorable sea conditions for comfortable travel in their top-heavy trawler.

At St. Thomas we prefer to anchor in the harbor of the capital, Charlotte Amalie, where the cruise ships come and go. Four giant ships arrive early each morning and depart each evening. It's quite a spectacle to enjoy the sunset from our cockpit while 200 yards in front of us a huge liner backs away from the dock, unassisted by tug boats, and heads out to sea with hundreds on board waving good-bye.

Fredericksburg neighbors Alice Gray Newcomb and Bill and Don Beckwith joined us in St. Thomas to sail in the British Virgin Islands. We had delightful stops at such exotic places as The Baths, where huge boulders have caused cave-like grottoes along one stretch of the shore of Virgin Gorda Island.

We anchored in Trellis Bay one afternoon, and dinghied to the tiny island in the middle of the bay for the buffet dinner and show at The Last Resort. Tony Snell, the British owner and entertainer kept us amused for over two hours with his ribald songs and his ever-changing facial expressions. Dogs, cats, goats and even a donkey named Vanilla roamed the open-air premises. We heard that Vanilla's predecessor, Chocolate, died of a liver ailment brought on by sipping too many of the customers' drinks.

We spent a night on a mooring at Sopers Hole, a pirates' anchorage from days of old. Off the beach at Deadman's Bay on Peter Island we anchored and went ashore by dinghy to spend an evening with Judy's cousins, Betsy and Dick Gaylord from Massachusetts, who were vacationing at the Peter Island Resort.

*   *   *   *   *

Over the Afloat Net radio/telephone hookup, we learned of our daughter Sally's engagement and pending marriage to Mark Barstow. We made plans to fly home from Panama for the April wedding before starting our Pacific crossing.

DASHING TO ARUBA
("John Miller"; beauty and the beach)

It has to be the fastest trip we have ever made by sailboat. El Yunque, the brooding mountain in the rain forest of Puerto Rico lingered on the horizon as we aimed for the island of Aruba, 440 nautical miles away. We knew the weather would be breezy and the sea swells large, but what we experienced exceeded our wildest imaginings. For sixty-eight hours we literally flew across the Caribbean Sea, barrelling along at 7.5 knots on a non-stop roller coaster. At times as we slid down the face of a large swell our speed indicator would read 9.5 knots!

There is traffic of all shapes and sizes in the Caribbean, the gateway to the Panama Canal. We passed a Russian trawler, several tankers and freighters, a cruise ship, and were even buzzed by a US Navy patrol plane on a drug surveillance mission.

We constantly thank God for "John Miller", our sturdy, reliable wind-steering device which can control CORMORANT even in the constant 25- to 35-knot winds we experienced. Only when the swells and wind drove us too far west did we have to manhandle the wheel.

The real John Miller is a burly, bearded, jolly fellow we met in Annapolis. He was interested in finding a boat like ours, and in exchange for a couple of sails on CORMORANT, he gave us thirty hours of his time and labor to help us install our Hydrovane system. We named our wind-steering system, which became a member of our crew, after him.

As dawn broke on the third day of our fast trip, Noordwest Punt, the northwest end of Aruba, lay directly ahead. We rounded it in winds up to 39 knots and the largest swells we had been in ....18 to 20 feet. Finally,

31

in the lee of the point, the wind eased to 25 knots and the swells subsided. We lowered our double-reefed mainsail and motored the remaining five miles to our anchorage near the capital of Oranjestad.

We were exhausted, but also delighted that the boat and crew had performed so well in this dash across the Caribbean. Everything worked, nothing broke, and though we were physically whipped, we felt an enormous sense of accomplishment.

*　*　*　*　*

Some of the real joys of cruising by sailboat are the arrivals, the anchorages, and the people you meet. Aruba was no exception. Two boats were already at the anchorage when we arrived, and in time we met Hjalmar and Kerstin (cruisers rarely use or remember last names) on GUNNICA IV and Tanil and Annette on KELEBEC.

On board our boat one evening we realized that five nations were represented among the crews of our three boats: Sweden, Norway, Turkey, Australia, and the U.S. GUNNICA IV left Scandinavia over a year ago on their way to the Pacific, and KELEBEC, from Turkey, had been around the world once and was going for seconds. We were finally meeting people who were doing what we were...going around the world.

*　*　*　*　*

ARUBA! The name conjures up thoughts of sun, sand, bright blue waters, strong winds, square coins, oil, and Carnival! Our timing was perfect, for our arrival at this Dutch island coincided with the annual pre-Lenten Carnival week.

Ashore we were impressed by the clean, pastel-colored city of Oranjestad. The warmth and hospitality of the people were contagious; everyone we met was happy,

32

courteous, and very helpful. The island license plate read: "One Happy Island", and we agreed.

Tourism is the biggest business in Aruba, with a major oil refinery on the south end of the island a close second. Clean public buses took us the length of the island for $1.50. In the town of San Nicholas we stopped for lunch at Charlie's Bar. Established in 1941, the right word to describe this locally renown watering hole is eclectic. We added our boat's calling card to the clutter on the wall and enjoyed tender Argentine beef you could cut with a fork.

For our last three days and nights, Carnival was the only thing on the minds of Arubans. We even noticed a sign on the door of the largest church in town: "Closed Sunday...Carnival!". From our anchorage, we felt and heard the beat of the ever-present music from the many bands that lined the streets.

With a parade every day or night of the week, we chose to watch the Grand Finale which went on for four hours on Sunday. Colorful floats and costumes, bands and dancers, paraded down the main street. The local Heineken beer distributor had the best advertisement .....a can of beer in the hand of each participant!

We finally said farewell to Aruba, where our last vision was of blonde, buxom Kerstin waving to us from the cockpit of GUNNICA IV, in the Swedish style.....topless.

MAGNIFICENT CARTAGENA
(European flavor amidst history and balmy climate)

Back on the ocean sailing to Cartagena, Colombia, we found the wind was still at 30 knots, and the seas huge. We kept a double reef in the mainsail and always wore our harnesses when in the cockpit. But the seas were at our back so it was not such a difficult trip.

We arrived at Cartagena after sixty-five hours on the ocean. Rounding the coast of Columbia, we imagined every dot on the radar to be some drug-smuggling boat out to take CORMORANT from us at gunpoint! To our enormous surprise and delight, Cartagena turned out to be the highlight of our trip so far. The people are sophisticated, the culture ancient, and the climate balmy.

Cartagena Bay reminded us of San Diego Bay, long and narrow. We entered at the southern entry, Boca Chica (small mouth), and motored an hour and a half to the smaller harbor just off the old city walls. The larger entry from the ocean, Boca Grande (large mouth), is impassable due to an underwater wall which was built across its wide opening as a deterrent to attackers of the past.

In fact, the great British Admiral, Edward Vernon (for whom Mount Vernon is named), failed to conquer Cartagena in 1741, due, in part, to that wall. The primary reason he failed was the skillful Spanish defense led by a peg-legged, one-armed, one-eyed Spanish Admiral, Don Blas de Lezo. It was a real thrill for us to sail in those same waters.

We anchored off Club Nautico, owned and operated for the last seventeen years by an Australian, Norman Bennett. Without question it was the most congenial, warm and welcoming marina we had been to. Norm runs it all on the honor system, with bills being brought current weekly. Again we met world cruisers; boats from San Francisco, England, Sweden, and Australia, to name a few. Some of these were cruising families who are raising and educating their children on board.

We walked the walls of this marvelous city, toured the cathedrals, climbed the massive Fortress of San Felipe, and visited the museum. Fresh flowers overflowed from window boxes on balconies and street corners. Past the old city, a newer section looked like Miami Beach, full of high-rise hotels and casinos.

The dollar-to-peso ratio makes prices very reasonable in Cartagena: beer...$0.50; lunch for two at a nice restaurant...$13.00. At the city center an International Film Festival was ongoing, and you could watch a first-run movie in English for $1.50.

Throughout our brief time in Cartagena, we felt perfectly safe walking around at night. We had the feeling of being in a hustling, bustling, old European city, very proud of its history, and equally proud of what it sees as the future..."the new destination". We were surprised and pleased that the drug situation of Colombia hasn't had a visible impact on this historic city.

All too soon we found ourselves on the ocean again, but now the seas were very moderate...four to six feet, and the wind had slacked to 15-20 knots, giving us a perfect two-day sail to Panama.

On arriving in Colon, probably the filthiest, most crime-ridden city in the Caribbean, we completed the first major leg of our trip around the world. With over 4,000 miles behind us, we were still confident of our boat, and were gaining more and more confidence in ourselves.

THE PANAMA CANAL
(A return visit to a modern-day wonder)

It has many names: The Big Ditch; The Path Between the Seas; The Bridge for the World...but no matter what it is called, the Panama Canal is one of the wonders of the world. Transiting the Canal by sailboat gave us a glimpse of the incredible challenge that was overcome in constructing this link between the Atlantic and Pacific Oceans.

We docked at the Panama Canal Yacht Club on the Atlantic side as we processed the required paperwork and awaited our transit day. One of the requirements was to pay all fees in cash (our fee was $125). When we explained that we had only travellers checks, a Panamanian official walked with us to a bank in Colon. Once Ward had the required money in his pocket the three of us were very vulnerable; we hurried back to the safety of the Canal area.

Sailboats must take two days to make the fifty-mile transit. In addition to the skipper, four line-handlers and a Panama Canal "advisor" are required for every boat. Our friend Bob Loe, who supervises the Navy-Marine Corps MARS program, joined us for the transit. Dwight Hite and Doug McMillan, soldiers from the US Army's airborne battalion in Panama, rounded out our crew. Our appointed "advisor", Thomas, linked up with us at our anchorage, and an hour later we were on our way.

There were thirty-five commercial ships and fourteen smaller boats representing over twenty countries scheduled to be in the Canal during our transit. The smaller boats travelled together into the locks. CORMORANT was the center boat in a raft of three sailboats. A Canadian boat, WAVE SWEEPER, headed to British Columbia, was on our left, and a French boat, OZ, sailing to Easter Island, was on our right. We lashed our boats together as we approached the first of three sets of locks. Each set consists of parallel locks, allowing ships to travel in opposite directions at the same time.

Even though we had been through the Canal several times (once in 1978 in our 23-foot sailboat, DOVE, when the transit fees were only $3.85) it is still intimidating to approach those massive locks. We crept in slowly until the lines to the outboard boats were secured to the wall. Then the enormous steel gates slowly swung shut behind us.

We were surrounded by fifty-foot high, slime-encrusted walls. The water started churning, as thousands of gallons from the freshwater lake above us were fed by gravity into the locks. As we rose, a huge cargo ship in the adjacent locks slowly descended.

When we had risen twenty-seven feet, the gates to the next chamber opened and the process was repeated. In three chambers, we rose eighty-five feet. We separated our raft when we were freed from the last chamber, and each boat followed the twisting channel along the twenty miles of Gatun Lake.

We unfurled our jib for this downwind trip, and motor-sailed past dozens of small islands in the man-made, fresh-water lake. After three hours of this idyllic travel, we anchored off the town of Gamboa, the midway point.

Our "advisor" went home for the night, while the crew had a refreshing swim, followed by dinner and talk of our day in the Panama Canal. A full moon rose, illuminating transiting ships which ghosted by during the night.

Thomas rejoined us at dawn, and we headed for the most spectacular part of the Canal; the Gaillard Cut. Here the passage narrowed to 100 yards as we approached the Continental Divide. Much of the effort during the ten years of construction of the Canal was expended here. Train loads of dirt were hauled twenty miles to the Pacific entrance of the Canal. There the dirt was dumped to build a causeway linking three small islands. The mountain was lowered an amazing 500 feet in this gigantic undertaking.

We squeezed to the right in the cut to allow a cruise ship to pass, then rafted our three boats again as we approached the Pedro Miguel Locks. Once secured to the walls of the locks, and with the gates shut behind us, the water of the chamber fed out, and we began to descend. In ten minutes the imposing gates in front of us opened; we were down to the level of Miraflores Lake.

We separated our raft, allowing CORMORANT to turn in to the Pedro Miguel Boat Club. The Canadian and French boats tied up to each other and approached the Miraflores Locks, a mile away. So that our crew could complete the entire Canal trip, Ward arranged for them to jump on board WAVE SWEEPER.

Our crew went down the two chambered locks at Miraflores, past the Port of Balboa, under the soaring arch of the Bridge of the Americas, to the Balboa Yacht Club. We chose to keep CORMORANT in the fresh water lake for the six weeks we would be in Panama. We thus avoided the salt water and the twenty-foot tidal difference that exists on the Pacific side.

Bob Loe headed back to Washington, D.C. and we took time to revisit many of our old haunts from fourteen years before when Ward was stationed in Panama with the US Army.

We left CORMORANT in good hands with our neighbor, Wally, who had lived on board his boat in Panama for twenty years, while we flew home to attend Sally and Mark's wedding. Two weeks later we were back on board preparing for the Pacific crossing.

Jauncey Sweet, Ward's brother-in-law from Fredericksburg, joined us for the trip from Panama to Tahiti. He's an experienced sailor and a great friend,

and we looked forward to having him share the challenges and joys of ocean sailing with us....especially the
night watches!

Leaving Annapolis
October 10th, 1991
Judy's dad, far left, gives a "thumbs up".

At sea enroute to the Virgin Islands

Ward puts a double reef in the mainsail

We exit Pedro Miguel Locks, Panama Canal

Jauncey Sweet at Miraflores Locks, Panama Canal

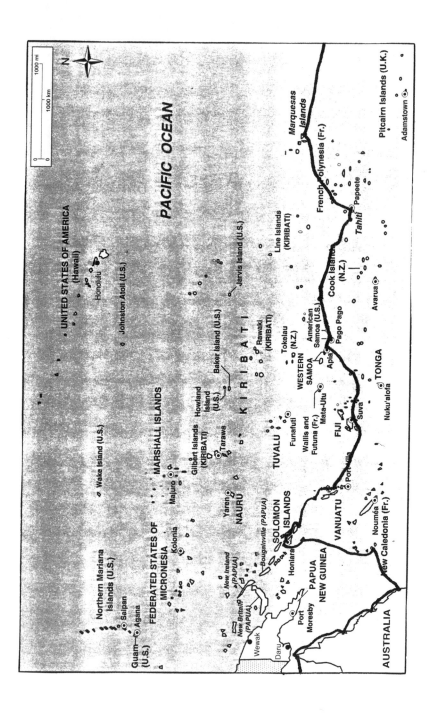

PANAMA TO TAHITI

"I must go down to the seas again,
to the lonely sea and the sky,
And all I ask is a tall ship
and a star to steer her by..."

From: "Sea-Fever"
by John Masefield

COCOS.....ISLE OF MYSTERY AND BEAUTY
(An idyllic stop in the vast Pacific Ocean)

Dolphins frolicked alongside us, some clearly visible through the blue water rushing under the bowsprit, as Cocos Island loomed ahead. We welcomed the soft brown gulls that circled overhead, seeming to escort us to their lush, green island.

*　　*　　*　　*　　*

We had left Panama six days earlier, three of us on board. After passing through the Miraflores locks of the Panama Canal we stopped for two days at the Balboa Yacht Club, which has moorings at the Pacific entrance to the Canal. It is adjacent to Fort Amador, where we had lived fourteen years before. Bullet holes still marked some of the buildings of Fort Amador where fighting occurred during "Operation Just Cause" in December of 1989.

Our final provisions were stuffed into all empty spaces on board, with extra jugs of water and fuel lashed to the deck. We knew this departure was significant since it would be months before we could find normal supplies and fuel...probably not until we reached Tahiti.

This departure also meant saying good-bye to many new friends we had made in our six weeks at the Pedro Miguel Boat Club:

..... Eric, the charming, toothless Panamanian who helped Ward do some major repairs to CORMORANT and whom we considered a real friend.

..... Wally, the affable Texan who lived aboard the boat next to us. His livelihood came from panning for gold in the streams of the Darien jungle along the Panama-Colombian border. He was an enormous help to us, driving us around Panama City finding last minute items, and even giving us an old anchor to use as a spare. We had him to dinner on board CORMORANT on our last night at Pedro Miguel*.

In Panama CORMORANT received a new bimini (canopy for our cockpit), extra support for the aluminum post our wind generator is mounted on, and a repaired Autohelm (our automatic steering system). Ward and Jauncey also installed our new G.P.S. (Global Positioning System...a push button location-finder which uses satellites), a surprise gift from members of the West Point Class of 1956. All these items were critical for this upcoming longest passage of our world trip...the Pacific.

*   *   *   *   *

We sailed out of the Bay of Panama in early May on good winds, then motored through two calm days, using our newly repaired Autohelm to steer. The winds then picked up to a steady 15 knots, bringing us the rest of the way to tiny Cocos Island. This island rises straight up out of the ocean, and is a jewel of black cliffs, waterfalls, and lush green rain forests.

Covering thirty square miles, three hundred miles offshore, Cocos is a Costa Rican National Park. There is one building on the island, a cottage that houses five park rangers. Two bays are suitable for anchoring; we chose Wafer Bay where we saw two other sailboats already at anchor.

Folklore has it that there is buried treasure on Cocos Island. The "Treasure of Lima" is said to have been hidden there in the 1820's, but the many expeditions to

---

* We would later learn that Wally was wanted for a murder he had committed twenty years earlier in Texas. Someone recognized him on the television show "Unsolved Mysteries", and he was arrested at Pedro Miguel Boat Club a year after we left.

find it have all failed.

Couples from the other boats dinghied over to meet us as we anchored, and at sunset we all gathered on board ARIETTE, owned by Mark and Laraine. They were heading for San Francisco as soon as they completed their three-year circumnavigation in French Polynesia in a month.

On our second day at Cocos we packed a picnic lunch and set out to find the treasure...the treasure of knowing a beautiful, unspoiled ocean island. We hiked up a marked trail into the lush forest. The trail followed a rushing stream, crossing it frequently, and we were kept busy choosing dry rocks for our footing. An occasional waterfall cascaded from the hill above us, and twice we stopped for a cool swim in the fresh, clear water. Smaller waterfalls along the stream created perfect "swimming pools" for us, where we also did our laundry. It was a weary but refreshed threesome that dinghied back to CORMORANT that afternoon.

After nearly two weeks away from grocery stores, we finally ate the last of our bread and Judy baked her first loaf in our tiny oven. Our supply of fresh fruits and vegetables, as well as the meat in the freezer, were gradually diminishing too, and for a while we would resort to canned and boxed goods.

We exchanged charts, books, and recipes when Klaus and Crystal from the adjacent boat RESTLESS came to call. They had lived aboard for three years, leisurely making their way from San Diego through Mexico to Cocos. The next morning as we weighed anchor, Klaus donned mask and snorkel and helped free our anchor chain from the rocks below.

As we sailed off towards the Galapagos Islands, Cocos was shrouded in rain-clouds....a haunting reminder of that magical yet mysterious island in the Pacific Ocean.

THE GALAPAGOS ISLANDS
(One of the last places where nature is untouched)

On the morning tide, just as the sun popped up in a cloudless sky, we glided into the harbor near Puerto Ayora. This small village at the end of Academy Bay, on the island of Santa Cruz, has become the center of activity in the Galapagos Islands. It was here that we would replenish some of our stores and take on water and fuel for our upcoming trip to French Polynesia, 3,000 miles and approximately thirty days away. We had crossed the Equator the day before, watching excitedly as "zero latitude" showed on our GPS.

*   *   *   *   *

Galapagos...the name means "giant tortoise" in Spanish...is one of the world's last remaining places where nature has not surrendered to progress. As we went ashore and later travelled across this island and others, we came to add another meaning... tranquility. The people are gentle and friendly; the hustle and bustle we saw in Panama had given way to a slower way of life. There is no noticeable crime, and the streets are spotlessly clean. Here we found a quiet, rustic, frontier style of living.

A visit to the Charles Darwin Research Station at the end of the main dirt street gave us a glimpse of "Lonesome George", one of the last of the gigantic tortoises. Painstaking efforts are being taken to reproduce and increase this endangered species in a natural, but controlled environment.

On one of the many docks along the water's edge we saw our first iguanas. Usually found dozing in the sun, these giant lizards are basically vegetarians, and relatively harmless, in spite of their ferocious look.

We ventured across the island by bus, rattling along a rocky dirt road, the only way from the town to the ferry landing and airport on the adjacent island of Baltra. There we boarded a small motor boat, LINDA, for a one hour trip to Las Plazas...the island home of a great horde of sea lions. What a treat to walk among these three-hundred pound monsters as they lazed by the sea.

Some pups were making noisy growling sounds to their mothers, who growled back, begrudgingly allowing another minute of feeding. We later swam and snorkeled nearby, and Jauncey came face to face underwater with a sea lion. It was mutual curiosity.

A winding path took us to the cliff's edge, where a hundred feet below the blue Pacific crashed among huge boulders. We were told by our guide that when the large male sea lions end a battle of supremacy over the flock of twenty-five female "cows", they lumber up these rocks to the top of the cliff where they rest and recuperate.

Blue-footed boobies, pelicans, iguanas and frigate birds, who dive bomb for fish from fifty feet in the air, abound in Las Plazas. Because of their protected status, all of these animals felt relatively comfortable with us in their midst. Even back at our anchorage, small yellow birds greeted us each morning with their beautiful warble and, with gentle encouragement, perched on our fingers.

The Galapagos Islands are part of Ecuador. Each of the major islands has a Port Captain, an Ecuadorian naval officer, who serves as the primary government authority on the island. Our Port Captain and his assistant, Freddie Macias, couldn't have been more helpful to us and other cruising sailors.

We needed thirty gallons of diesel fuel and eighty gallons of fresh water to top off our tanks and spare containers. Freddie, using the few English words he knows, said, "No problem!" and proceeded to deliver containers of water and fuel by launch to our anchored boat. We paid all costs, and provided beer, CORMORANT tee-shirts, and hats as a way of saying thanks to the sailors who helped us.

We would have taken CORMORANT to more of these islands, but the Ecuadorian government restricts private boats to only one island; the rest must be visited by tour boat. Permission can be obtained to sail to other islands, but it takes about two years to arrange, and often the paperwork is lost.

We felt very content in getting to know the island of Santa Cruz and some of the people of Puerto Ayora in our five days here. Henry, a friendly German who operated Henry's Snack Bar, had been there twenty years. He was always sitting in the same chair and had helpful advice to anyone who stopped. Jack Nelson, a yachtsman from California, owned the Hotel Galapagos, the American hangout in town. He has been there off and on for twenty-two years, and helped us with mail and laundry.

Jauncey injured his finger, so we stopped by the only hospital in town to get medical attention. Since Ecuador is on a socialized medicine program, the doctor gave thirty minutes of treatment at no cost.

Soon we were off for the longest stretch of our trip without land, from the Galapagos Islands to the Marquesas in French Polynesia. We left with a warm feeling for the people we had met, and for the very gentle way in which nature and man are working together to preserve a way of life that is unique.

SAILING THROUGH WITH FLYING COLORS
(3,000 miles; night watches, dolphin, starlit skies)

Forbidding grey clouds blanketed the sky. The ocean became mountains of dark swells, some as high as a two-story building. These huge seas glided under our stern to lift us up then swoosh us down into the trough between waves. The air was warm, but we were in foul weather jackets, fending off the spray of breaking waves and the rain. We were well into our first week out of the Galapagos Islands, in steady 20- to 30-knot winds, waiting for the gentle trade winds. Our wind generator happily whirled away, keeping CORMORANT's four batteries fully charged.

Two and a half years before, we had chosen our boat based on its ability to sustain this leg of the trip. The boat had to be able to store enough water, fuel, and food for this thirty-day passage. It had to be sturdy enough to withstand wind and waves under all conditions, and comfortable enough for us to enjoy living aboard. COR-MORANT passed those tests with flying colors during this our longest passage at sea.

The three of us quickly settled into a routine that would last only twenty-two days. Because of good winds in the early part of our trip, when we zipped along under a double-reefed mainsail at 6.5 knots, we cut our expected time at sea by almost a week. We stood three-hour watches, giving each of us six hours off to rest between watches. To help pass the time we listened to tapes on the "Walkman", read, and slept.

A constant source of balance in this topsy-turvy existence was our radio/telephone contact. Through the Navy-Marine Corps MARS Afloat Net, we placed three or four calls a week to family and friends. In short bursts of conversation, followed by the word "over", we kept them aware of our location and they kept us up to date on events back home.

We also joined in a twice-a-day radio net with seven other boats making this long passage, boosting each other's morale even though we never saw any of those boats at sea. In fact, we saw only one ship on this part of the Pacific Ocean.

The immensity of this trackless ocean is hard to capture in words. We never let it bother us, but later learned that one boat in our net had real problems coping with the total isolation. For us, the stars became our night companions; the Big Dipper on our right and the Southern Cross on our left.

Often we would troll for our dinner, hooking two dorados and a three-foot eel. We ate the dorados and let the eel go. We were surprised that birds were often around, even when we were a thousand miles from land. The highlight of our days at sea was the evening meal, where Judy never ceased to amaze us with yet another original hot concoction.

Halfway into our trip our morale sagged when the propane gas stove wouldn't ignite. For three days in rolling seas we suffered along with cold meals, trying to find the problem. Finally we removed the stove, to discover a severed electrical wire. With the wire mended, our spirits soared as we went back to having hot meals.

After covering two-thirds of our distance, we finally caught the trade winds and had sunny skies. We were able to sail "wing and wing" directly before the prevailing east winds. With more than a week left in our trip, passing that point gave us all a lift, and somehow it seemed that land was just over the horizon. As the miles sailed by, we set our clocks back one hour every 900 miles, until we were six hours behind the East Coast of the U.S.

At midday on our twenty-second day at sea we spotted land...the island of Mohotani, thirty miles away. We scanned the distant horizon for more islands of the Marquesas chain, and Hiva Oa (our destination) and Tahuata slowly emerged from the haze.

It was thrilling to know that we were exactly where we thought we were, thanks to the wizardry of our GPS, and that civilization was just a few hours away. A school of more than fifty bottle-nosed porpoise joined us for a dazzling display of leaps and dives. Once four of them leapt completely out of the water in unison, better than any chorus line could do.

We decided to motor the remaining miles in hopes of making our anchorage in daylight. But night comes quickly in the South Pacific, and we found ourselves approaching land well after dark. Normally we would wait offshore for daylight, but some of our sailing friends were already in the harbor ready to guide us in, and after twenty-two days at sea, we were anxious.

With excellent charts, our radar, and a full moon rising, we continued on. Ironically, a total eclipse blacked out the moon just when we reached the harbor. The lighted cross on the hill overlooking the harbor remained our constant beacon and helped to guide us safely in.

We anchored easily and began to experience the feeling that overwhelms anyone who successfully accomplishes something demanding and challenging. In the dark of night we began putting faces with the voices who had kept us company on the radio for the past three weeks. New friends dinghied over to help us set our anchors and share in the joy of a safe passage completed. The soft lilt of the French language wafted over the calm waters from other boats, confirming that we were in French Polynesia...three weeks and a world apart from Galapagos.

GAUGUIN'S PARADISE
(A memorable stop in French Polynesia)

Nuku Hiva, Fatu Hiva, Hiva Oa....until now these were only exotic names we'd read in books. These lovely islands in the French Marquesas were about to come to life for us, just as they did for James Michener, Herman Melville, Thor Hyerdahl, and so many others.

We awoke on the morning of June 15th and rushed to the cockpit to see Atuona Harbor in Hiva Oa, our new home. Lush tropical foliage, with a profusion of wild-looking palm trees, grew up the steep banks of the narrow basin we shared with twelve other boats. Looking back to where we had entered the night before, we saw the larger Traitor's Bay, backed by sharp purple cliffs in the distance.

High above the harbor loomed a mountain with jagged cliffs and a constantly rain-shrouded summit. A crude cement dinghy dock and a couple of buildings lay on the shore nearby. A larger commercial dock, used by the weekly supply boat from Tahiti, was near the harbor entrance, just inside the small breakwater.

Lee Sharon, an American single-hander on QUEST, rowed over to show us the way ashore. At the cement dock high tide can cause a difficult if not impossible landing, so cruisers preferred pulling their dinghies up on a little rocky beach, in a tiny inlet hidden by trees.

With our dinghy, PING, safely pulled up the rocks and tied to a palm tree, we began the hike up the tree-lined road towards the village of Atuona. A friendly young Polynesian woman came along in her jeep and offered us a ride, saving us the two-mile hike to town.

Our first destination was "The Snack Bar", a brightly decorated open-air establishment that is the favorite local gathering place for breakfast and lunch. Over coffee

53

and flaky French croissants, we planned our day, and soon other sailors joined us for beers to celebrate our arrival.

After changing our money into Polynesian francs we paid our compulsory visit to the "Gendarmerie", to check in with the authorities. Stringent laws regulate the length of stay for cruisers and their yachts, but the agreeable tee-shirted Polynesian behind the desk did not seem to care where we went or how long we stayed, so long as we filled out all of his forms.

A stroll the length of the village took all of fifteen minutes. The narrow, roughly paved streets were bordered with hedges bearing hibiscus blossoms of all hues of red and coral, and friendly school girls with flowers in their long black hair smiled readily and said "hello" wherever we went.

The stores and offices close down between noon and 2:00 p.m., so we had a leisurely lunch at the "Snack Bar". The typical island fare is a delicious stir-fry of meat or seafood and fresh vegetables, served over noodles or rice.

Later we found the three stores in town. Prices being extremely high, we purchased only some Coca-Cola and baguettes, the long, thin loaves of French bread.

That night the crews from four of the boats that had been in radio contact throughout our journey across the Pacific gathered at the one real restaurant in town to get acquainted over a delicious seafood dinner and fine French wine. Patsy and Chris, a British couple on JALINGO III, whom we had met at the Galapagos, Bob and Toni from Australia, about to complete a circumnavigation, and their friend, Bob, who is sailing this leg with them aboard QUEST II, and Lee from QUEST (no relation) rounded out our group.

We remained at Hiva Oa for four days, time enough to rest and prepare for departure. Taken aback to see murky brown scum and green sea moss partly obliterating CORMORANT's sharply painted water line, Ward spent two hours scrubbing the hull clean. Judy wiped down the interior of the boat, which had acquired a damp, salty film.

Judy and Jauncey hand-washed our huge pile of laundry at a spigot by the dinghy dock, enjoying the abundant flow of cool, clear mountain water. Soon our boat, and others around us, looked like a floating laundry, with clothes drying on every available line.

A cement shower stall, where water came in a single rush out of a crude pipe, stood out in the open, adjacent to the washing spigot. Some island people, as well as boaters, took advantage of this "luxury".

Before we sailed off, we returned to town to check out with the authorities and visit Hiva Oa's main attraction, the grave of French Impressionist painter, Paul Gauguin. Up a winding road we climbed in the hot sun to the local cemetery, where a simple tomb had "Paul Gauguin" roughly carved in a rounded lava rock at the foot. Plumaria trees encircled the spot, sending down an occasional fragrant yellow blossom. A well known French singer, Jacques Brel, is buried nearby.

The morning we left Hiva Oa we pulled up to the commercial dock at high tide to fill our water tanks, not an easy maneuver in bouncy seas by a rough cement wall. Our friends all left later for the island of Nuku Hiva, to take on diesel fuel or pick up mail, while we set sail for Fatu Hiva, an easy day's sail away.

*   *   *   *   *

The Bay of Virgins on Fatu Hiva is said to be one of the most beautiful spots in all of French Polynesia. We were not disappointed. We arrived just after dark on a clear night and dropped anchor in forty feet of water among five other boats.

A stunning sight met our eyes at dawn; we were anchored between sheer lava cliffs, some with enormous volcanic plugs protruding upwards. Beyond were steep verdant mountains where a few goats and cows grazed. At the end of this very narrow bay was the small village of Hanavave, tucked behind the rocky beach in a wild abundance of palm trees along a swift mountain stream.

In the center of the village stood a blue and white wooden church. The missionaries had done a great job here, for around every neck we saw a cross of some type. We were at Fatu Hiva on Father's Day, and were surprised to learn that it was also recognized in Polynesia. Except for a small opening in a solid wall of lava a hundred feet high, the village was sealed off from the distant valley. It reminded us of the "King Kong" movie set.

Outrigger canoes (made of fiberglass and powered by outboard engines!) came out to greet us, and began the custom unique to islands where there is no airstrip; bartering. Money was never involved as we traded fish hooks, tee shirts, shotgun shells, lipsticks, and packs of garden seeds for freshly caught fish and fruit.

Papaya, bananas, limes, grapefruit and mangoes over-flowed onto our boat, as we quickly fell in love with this place and the warm, gracious, curious, very independent, and surprisingly well-educated Polynesians of Fatu Hiva.

We spent only two nights at the Bay of Virgins, then started a six-day sail to the Tuamotus atolls. Two days beyond that we would reach Tahiti; that classic South Pacific gem, where two months of mail awaited us.

TAHITI...SOUTH SEAS PARADISE
(Island sunsets and much more)

For most, Tahiti is synonymous with all that is magical about the South Seas. We were enchanted with the climate, the people, the tropical lushness of the island, and the laid-back energy that abounds in Papeete, the capital.

*   *   *   *   *

Before our long awaited rest and repair stop in Tahiti, we sailed through the Tuamotus, a series of ancient, low-lying atolls. We stopped at Rangiroa, the largest atoll, timing our arrival to pass through the narrow opening in the coral reef on the incoming tide.

Once in the lagoon, we joined other boats anchored off the Kia-Ora Hotel. We snorkeled off a small island in an area known locally as "the aquarium". There a kaleidoscope of iridescent colors flashed by us as fish swarmed around to take bread right from our hands. Reef sharks and huge Moray eels were visible nearby, though only the smaller fish surrounded us to nibble....thank goodness!

During our two-day sail from Rangiroa to Tahiti the clew (grommet to which the sheet, or securing line, is attached) of our large genoa ripped out. Earlier, a thousand miles from Tahiti, corrosion had caused a break in our gooseneck (the aluminum bracket where the boom and the mast connect), more of an inconvenience than a catastrophe. Both would be repaired in Tahiti for less than $200, but now, with considerably shortened sails, we still barrelled along at 5 knots in a 20-knot breeze.

We entered Papeete harbor just after dark, and easily found the well-lit anchorage. During daylight, we lined up with the other boats "Med-moored" in front of the Paofai Temple, with an anchor off our bow, and two stern lines tied off to palm trees.

Our timing was perfect, for we were in Papeete during the annual *Fete* ....a two-month long celebration highlighted by outrigger canoe races, dance contests and a carnival. The Tamure, the traditional Tahitian dance, is a more violent and throbbing version of the gentle, swaying Hawaiian Hula.

During *Fete*, dance troupes of more than 100 men and women, representing the island groups in French Polynesia, competed as they shook to the incessant staccato of the drum-beat. Dressed in colorful native costumes, the women shake their hips rapid-fire, while the men shake their knees, both with arms gracefully outstretched for balance as they follow their dance routine in the sand.

We took a quick side trip to Moorea early in our stay in Tahiti. Jauncey had to catch his plane back to the States after ten weeks and more than 5,000 miles logged as our always cheerful crew member. Before he left, we wanted him to see this "Bali Hai"-island fifteen miles to the west.

After a quick three-hour sail, we moored to a tree in the picture-postcard Opunohu Bay, with the jagged peaks of Moorea towering above us. We joined Nick and Pat Ellison and their family on another American boat, LUSTY WIND, anchored nearby, for a pot-luck Fourth of July celebration. After dark we gathered on deck to shoot off a couple of flares and sing the Star Spangled Banner under a perfect, tropical, star-spangled sky.

On Bastille Day, July 14th, the French military marched down the street fronting the water in Papeete. Included were elements from the elite French Foreign Legion, as well as Army and Navy units. This is the center of French military presence in the Pacific, which includes a Nuclear Test Site on one of the more remote atolls 800 miles to the southeast. The waterfront was a colorful sight that day, as all sailboats were asked to "dress ship", stringing their many signal flags from the bow to mast-top to stern.

Riding a local bus, called *Le Truck*, we went to the Paul Gauguin museum on the opposite side of Tahiti. It was fascinating to trace the troubled life of this French Impressionist painter whose most famous works depict Tahitian life.

We decided to hitch-hike around the rest of island, a very accepted means of transportation among these gentle, friendly people. A young Tahitian named Marc Ropati offered us a ride and showed us the sights along the remaining fifty miles of the perimeter road. We watched canoe races taking place near a small village and had a breathtaking view of the island from a spot high up a mountain.

We invited Marc, his wife, Augustine, and their two children to our boat. They brought us bananas, pine-apples, breadfruit, avocados, and limes from their fields. In a combination of languages we assured each other that we would stay in touch.

A visit to Papeete isn't complete without a visit to *Les Trucks*. Along the docks in the evening, ten or fifteen trucks pull in, open up their sides, set out bar stools, and provide the best and least expensive meal in town. Everything from crepes to pizza, ice cream to coffee, egg rolls to chop suey can be found at *Les Trucks*.

We also found Lou Pescadou's pizza house, where, if there was a waiting line, drinks were on the house until you were seated. The cook, Mario, entertains while cook-ing, with his loud, off-key singing. The three times we ate there we found the place packed, but never had to wait for a red-checkered table.

*   *   *   *   *

While Papeete and Tahiti are the hub of commerce and activity in the South Pacific, the history of this part of the world also centers here. Most theories have Tahitians as the courageous sea voyagers who first discovered and populated the Marquesas Islands, the Tuamotos, the Cook Islands, and the Hawaiian Islands.

Though that adventuresome spirit seems to have been tamed by the good life, we were impressed with the strength of character, strong family bonds, and healthy independence exhibited by the Tahitians we met. It is also the first place we've seen in the Pacific where a variety of religions coexist, and the churches are packed on Sundays.

We were captivated by these smiling, happy people. Mix in the warm, gentle climate, and exotic, breathtaking scenery, and you quickly see why so many come to Tahiti and never leave.

FRENCH POLYNESIA

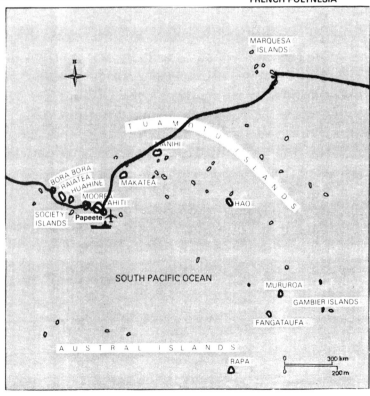

FAREWELL TO FRENCH POLYNESIA
(Polynesian graciousness, French aristocracy)

The half-moon hung in the cloudless midnight sky, like a pale slice of lemon. We followed its radiance, a shimmering silver river on a blackened sea, our pathway out of French Polynesia. Soon the moon dipped below the horizon, and the sky came ablaze with a billion lights. We ghosted past the last darkened atoll, 170 miles west of Bora Bora, and quietly, sadly said farewell to these exotic isles.

Ahead lay 500 miles of ocean to an isolated spit of land called Suvarov Atoll in the northern Cook Islands, then another 400 miles to American Samoa. These distances remind us of just how immense is the Pacific Ocean.

*   *   *   *   *

Eight days earlier we had departed the bustling harbor of Papeete after a stay of several weeks. We spent a few days at picturesque Cook's Bay on the nearby island of Moorea, where the Bali Hai Club offered yachters use of their pool and other facilities. We circled Moorea on a Vespa motorscooter, enjoying an elevated view of the bay, and a white sandy beach looking back to Tahiti across fifteen miles of ocean.

If you have only one island to visit in all of French Polynesia, it should be Bora Bora. After an overnight sail from Moorea, past the islands of Huahini, Raiatea, and Tahaa, this green jewel set in an azure sea beckoned us from our first glimpse thirty miles away.

Bora Bora's reef, with thundering breakers trailing smoking plumes of spray, completely encircles the lagoon and the island with its soaring mountain. Once

through the only pass and inside the wide lagoon, COR-
MORANT sailed on blue, crystal clear waters. James
Michener described Bora Bora as the Pacific's most beau-
tiful island, and we agree.

We lingered at Bora Bora for four days, renting bicycles one day to circle the entire island. Along the way
we strolled through the luxurious Bora Bora Hotel and
stopped to see Bloody Mary's, an open-air restaurant
which proudly boasts having hosted a long list of celebrities, from Prince Rainier to Jimmy Buffett. Pedalling
leisurely past miles and miles of beautiful beach and
occasional dwellings and hotels, we returned to our starting point five hours later.

The only real village on Bora Bora, Vaitape, had a
series of thatch-roofed temporary booths along the waterfront for the summer-long *Heiva* festival. Good smells
of snacks cooking and the sound of loud music seemed
to continue there day and night.

More appealing than the bustling carnival on Tahiti
with its rides and games, this rural atmosphere showed
us another side of French Polynesia. The champion
"Tamure" dancers of Bora Bora, just back from the final
competition on Tahiti, danced nightly in the village
square. When we tied up to the town dock one afternoon to purchase some supplies we were visited by a
collection of curious, friendly young boys, who watched
the boat for us while we shopped.

The Bora Bora Yacht Club offered free moorings, ri-
diculously high-priced laundry service, and excellent
French cuisine. Included in the atmosphere were the
owner's grandchildren running around underfoot and
dogs begging for bites of our meals! After one night there
we opted for a quiet anchorage near a small island inside the reef, where we swam and snorkeled and visited
with Toni and Bob on QUEST II. We spent our final
night at Bora Bora swinging on the mooring that Bloody
Mary's offers, rowing ashore to enjoy lobster caught on

the reef the night before.

Back at the Yacht Club dock to fill our water tanks, we realized how void we were of current information when we learned from a visiting Australian about the U.S. Presidential campaign. We were told President Bush was lagging in the polls. From this distance, the issues, other than the slump in the worldwide economy, were not clear. In any case, we will always side with strength of character, and planned to cast our absentee votes for George Bush.

With Bora Bora behind us, we sailed smartly towards the west. Alone now, we establish a four-hour watch schedule. Two days out we were still brisking along in 20 knots of wind as we headed northwest towards the northern Cook Islands. QUEST II, sailing ahead of us, opted to turn southwest towards Rarotonga in the southern Cook Islands.

In our twice-a-day radio checks we learned on our third day out that QUEST II was in 35-knot winds and high seas. This storm system would reach us two days later, but lasted only eighteen hours. Our friends were in the thick of it for three days. As a result, Toni flew home to Australia from Rarotonga, and Bob signed on two crew members to help him finish their six-year circumnavigation. We planned to see Bob and Toni again when we reached Australia.

As we reflected on French Polynesia several thoughts stood out. The islands are truly spectacular. The nice blend of Polynesian graciousness and French aristocracy make for a delightful combination: efficient but with a South Seas' *savoir faire* attitude. The prices were outrageous, however, and for that reason alone it was time to move on. We still had 3,000 miles to go to reach Australia, and only four months before the cyclone season would begin in the South Pacific.

Galapagos at lunchtime

Galapagos Iguanas

At sea crossing the Pacific

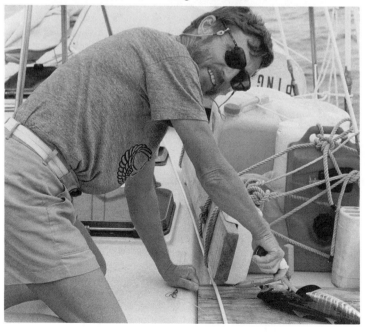

Ward cuts up a fish for dinner

Laundry day in Marquesas Islands

Judy bakes bread as we sail across the Pacific

BORA BORA TO AUSTRALIA

"Eternal Father, strong to save,
Whose arm hath bound the restless wave,
Who bidd'st the mighty ocean deep
Its own appointed limits keep:
O hear us when we cry to thee
For those in peril on the sea."

1st verse from the Navy Hymn,
"Eternal Father, Strong to Save"
by William Whiting

SUWARROW ATOLL
(Home of Tangi-Jimmy, a living legend)

The guide books on Polynesia say that the northern Cook Islands are "out of tourist range". Thankfully so! We broke up our 1,000-mile sail between Bora Bora and Pago Pago, American Samoa with a stop at Suvarov Atoll. Russian explorer Mikhail Lazarev first spotted the atoll in 1814, and named it for his ship, the SUVAROV. The name has since taken on a different spelling to fit the Polynesian pronunciation.... Suwarrow.

We almost decided not to sail the fifty miles off our rhumb line to Pago Pago to reach Suwarrow, but the past twenty-four hours had been exceptionally rough. We were hammered by 30-knot winds, twelve-foot seas, and heavy rains in the most severe weather we had seen since we left Panama.

We dropped anchor at Anchorage Island (the largest spot of land on the atoll) just as the last glow of the day was replaced by the light of the full moon. Too exhausted to enjoy the view, we ensured our boat was anchored securely then crashed into a deep sleep.

The next sound we heard was a knock on the hull and a cheerful, "Good Morning". As Judy arose to see who it was, a boat sped away. A native woman in the boat yelled back, "Fish for you!", pointing to our boat. We found a beautiful ten-pound amberjack on our deck.

That was our introduction to an amazing story that is being lived out on this small atoll in the middle of the South Pacific...the story of Tangi-Jimmy and Suwarrow.

*   *   *   *   *

Suwarrow Atoll has long been an island of dreams. At different times in this century two reclusive misfits sought to "get away from it all" there.

In the 1920's, an American named Robert Dean Frisbie drifted north from Tahiti to Manihiki and Puka Islands. There he gained a native wife and four children. Disillusioned after his wife's early death, Frisbie moved with his four children to Suwarrow in the mid-1930's, where he hoped to live off the land and sea in splendid isolation.

In February 1942, unaware the world was at war, Frisbie had his own war...with a devastating hurricane. On the night of 19 February, Frisbie, his four children, three land surveyors, and three native workers from Manihiki tied themselves to the strongest limbs of the largest tamanu tree in the center of this tiny island. The force of wind and sea sounded like a freight train, and at the height of the storm the ocean covered the island with six feet of water. But everyone survived. One of the natives tied to that tree was Tangi-Jimmy's father.

New Zealander Tom Neale claimed Suwarrow as his isle of dreams from 1952 to 1977. Here, on this deserted atoll, Neale planned to live out his life as a hermit. With visiting yachts, land surveyors, and fishing vessels blown off course by storms, Tom was never isolated for long. He gained a reputation for being totally charming to his frequent visitors. Although he left the island for brief periods for health reasons, he lived at Suwarrow for sixteen years until he died of cancer in 1977 at the age of seventy-five.

In the mid 1980's, the Cook Island government decided to make Suwarrow a National Park. Tangi-Jimmy, whose father had come close to death in the 1942 hurricane, moved to the island in 1986 as the Island Administrator. This large and gentle man eventually moved his family to Suwarrow, and then more Tangi relatives joined until now three adults and four children live on this special island.

Manekino (Mama), Jimmy's wife, holds center-stage

for this expanding family. Well into her sixties, she is a fine, cultured woman who in the early days at Suwarrow longed for her friends and a more active social life. Often she would say, "Maybe we should move to Manihiki where our friends are all making fortunes growing black pearls?" Jimmy would answer, "Yes, Mama, but they lie, cheat, and steal to make a profit; and none of them are happy. Here we have everything we need. And we are living the life that only riches are supposed to bring!" Mama now seems content at Suwarrow, especially with four of her twenty-two grandchildren in sight.

Under a huge tamanu tree, she delights in talking for hours to visiting yachtsmen about the Tangi family and Suwarrow. The Cook Islands once belonged to New Zealand, so English was spoken as we sat around.

Jimmy's son, William, had been the Immigration Officer at Suwarrow until just recently. Twenty-one years old, William had no real aim in life, but at Suwarrow something happened. Maybe it was the isolation, the closeness to nature, the wind and sea, the thousands of birds and fish, the constantly swaying coconut palms or the empty horizon beyond the reef. Whatever it was, Jimmy was bursting with pride as he told us that William was on his way to Hawaii to enter the priesthood of the Catholic Church.

Frances, William's sister, had agreed to move to Suwarrow to replace him as the "Immigration Officer". She wasn't happy working as a nurse in Rarotonga, while her two sons, Larry (6), and Hiriaki (3), were being raised by their grandparents on Suwarrow. Jimmy had sought to have the children on this island paradise while they were young; perhaps as a lure for Frances, a single parent, but more than likely to see that they were raised to respect God and nature as a way of life.

You'd think that teenagers would become restless on this tiny island. Not so with fourteen year old Sophie and thirteen year old Naomi, two outgoing and poised young girls. Their mother lives in Rarotonga and helps to coordinate the shipment of supplies for Suwarrow.

Naomi met us on our first visit ashore with a glass of coconut milk while we filled out the immigration and customs forms for the Cook Islands. Later, when we completed an hour's walk around the island, Sophie served us delicious coconut pancakes which she had cooked on an open coconut-husk fire in the outdoor kitchen.

Children and adults alike from other boats played with the four children and became members of the Tangi family as long as they were at Suwarrow. As we left, it became obvious that we would forever be members of the extended Tangi family. Our last session with Jimmy and Mama under the tamanu tree, our conversation turned to God.

We had been surprised to see a small, makeshift chapel inside the house, and learned that Jimmy conducted church services every Sunday. He invites all visiting boaters, and after church hosts a fish-fry on the beach. Normally, all crew members, no matter what their faith, attend. We learned that Jimmy was authorized by the Catholic Bishop of Polynesia to administer the sacraments during Mass.

We gave the family some things from our boat that we knew they needed: soap, paper products, macaroni, magazines, shampoo, crayons and canned meat. We walked away with coconuts, pancakes, and large mother-of-pearl shells. Naomi stretched to her full height to place shell leis around each of our necks.

With hugs and handshakes we left, carrying their guest book back to CORMORANT. They asked that we write something and include our picture. Mama was pleased to tell us that ultimately the guest books which the Tangi family have been keeping will be placed in the Cook Island Museum on Rarotonga.

At dawn on the day of our departure, Jimmy was at

our boat. He had just returned through the pass to the lagoon with five beautiful amberjacks, and one was for us. As we returned the guest book we realized that through his kindness and example he is spreading God's word. His family reflects it, the cruisers who visit here feel it, and the history of this island atoll will chronicle it.

We raised our anchor and slowly motored around the island and out of the lagoon. Hoisting our sails and turning into the wind to enter the pass to the ocean, we took one last look and there on the beach, waving farewell with a huge towel, was Jimmy, the living legend of Suwarrow.

A TALE OF TWO SAMOAS
(The worst of the modern, the best of the traditional)

Pago Pago (pronounced "Pango Pango"), on the island of Tutuila in American Samoa, is reputed to be the finest natural harbor in the South Pacific. Bustling with the arrival of container ships, fishing boats, yachts, and the twenty-four hour operation of two Tuna canneries, this formerly serene, yet still picturesque spot has seen great changes in recent years.

Our friend Judy Housley, from Annapolis, was waiting on the dock when we arrived. She came here to be our crew member for two weeks and also to reminisce. More than fifty years ago, when she was twelve, her naval officer father was Aide to the Governor of American Samoa.

Now, the pristine Navy Yard and the line of comfortable, veranda-trimmed quarters along "Centipede Row", where her family lived, were gone. In their place stood stacks of colorful shipping containers four high and ten deep, and piles of huge commercial fishing nets awaiting repair. Fifty years ago the harbor was perfect for swimming; now it is filthy. The U.S. Navy left Pago Pago in the early 1950's, and the Department of the Interior now oversees this totally different scene.

After having visited many ports over the last eight months, we found Pago Pago appalling. Only Colon and Balboa in Panama were worse for filth, apathetic administrators, and cumbersome bureaucratic nonsense heaped on arriving yachts. We had been anxious to show off "America" to our foreign yachting friends as they arrived in Pago Pago; instead, we kept a low profile and sought out competent local authorities to whom we offered our constructive comments.

No matter how much Pago Pago has changed over

the years, for a sailing yacht, arriving after more than a week at sea, it offers a much-needed rest-stop. The grocery stores are stocked with longed-for American products at decent prices, and, best of all, there is a U.S. Post Office. As soon as our provisioning was complete, with Judy Housley at the helm, we set out for Apia, the capital of Western Samoa, an overnight sail.

Waiting for us there was Vai Ala'ilima, a Samoan family chief, or "matai", and Member of Parliament, ready to spend a week showing us around. His engaging smile and gentle nature readily captivated us. Judy, our guest, had renewed her acquaintance with Vai quite by accident a year earlier, when visiting Samoa on an "Elderhostel".

Western Samoa gained independence from New Zealand in 1962. Although it is clearly a Third World country, this proud nation retains its ancient customs, such as the communal ownership of land by the "aiga", or family group, of which the "matai" is head. Most notable is the continuation of "fa'a Samoa", or the Samoan way of generosity and hospitality.

Clad in his "lavalava" (a cloth tied loosely around the waist, in lieu of trousers), short-sleeved cotton shirt, and rubber thongs, Vai drove us around in his well-used pickup truck. Fay, his American or "pulagi" (foreign) wife of forty years, whom he had met in Washington, D.C. while completing his Master's Degree at American University, was in Hawaii visiting a daughter. We were sorry not to meet her but did read her two excellent books, *My Samoan Chief*, about her husband and the Samoan way of life, and *Aggie Grey, a Samoan Saga*.

CORMORANT was anchored in the quiet, relatively clean harbor of Apia, in front of the legendary Aggie Grey's Hotel. The hotel grew from a hamburger stand operated during World War II for American troops by the engaging, enterprising Aggie Gray. Three years before her death in 1988, at the age of ninety, Aggie was still known to close the hotel's weekly floor show with her stunning and dignified version of the Samoan "Siva" dance. The "Siva" is a gentle, almost imperceptible heel and toe movement across the floor with graceful arms and hands telling a story. Aggie gained unwelcome fame when it was falsely reported that James Michener used her as his inspiration for "Bloody Mary" in his Tales of the South Pacific.

Early one morning with Vai leading the way, we hiked up Mount Vaea, behind the town of Apia, to the tomb of Robert Louis Stevenson. Vai brought along four coconuts which he deftly cut open with his machete when we reached the top. They were the coolest, most refreshing drink and snack imaginable after our hour-long hike.

Almost a hundred years after his death, the poem used in Stevenson's gravestone epitaph is still taught worldwide in high school English Literature classes:

"Home is the sailor home from the sea
And the hunter home from the hill."

At the end of our hike we cooled off in a stream under the natural outdoor "shower" Stevenson himself had used.

Church attendance is important in this Christian nation. On Sunday we went to a small church where nearly the whole congregation was part of Vai's extended family. All Samoans wear white to church, the men in coat and tie with tailored "lavalava", and the women in long, flowing dresses. Dozens of children, also clad in white, sang robustly and in beautiful harmony, as did their elders. The service was followed by a lavish pot-luck feast served as we sat on floor mats in Vai's sister's *fale* (pronounced "fahlay"), a typical open-air Samoan house, next door.

On another day in Western Samoa, we met Vai at

Aggie Grey's Hotel dinghy dock before dawn. Piling into his pickup truck with overnight bags, we began an unforgettable thirty-six hour excursion. On the far side of the island of Upolu, we caught a ferryboat for the hour-long ride to the large island of Savai'i, the ancestral home of all Samoans. During our eight-hour sightseeing ride around that island, we saw dozens of huge churches, and friendly, happy people. At one unexpected stop, an entire school of children stopped what they were doing, faced the road, and sang us a song.

We finally stopped at the village of Samata. They were expecting us and immersed us in *fa'a Samoa*, the Samoan way of life. After the traditional and solemn *Kava* (a strong, bitter root drink) welcoming ceremony, which we are told is seldom witnessed by visitors, Vai presented many small monetary gifts to the local chiefs as we all sat cross-legged on the floor. He also gave cases of flour, biscuits and canned fish to the village. The villagers presented us with finely woven mats, shell necklaces, and a freshly killed pig.

The women of the village prepared a huge feast for us, and then entertained us with traditional singing and dancing. Children were allowed to stay up to watch; their faces shone with excitement, especially when we three *pulagis* had to dance the *Siva*.

The church and the preacher's home, a modest two-story house where we slept, are the focus of any Samoan village. A year before, this four bedroom house had held over three hundred villagers for five days as they regrouped following the devastation of Hurricane Val.

Judy Housley left us in Apia, and we concluded our time in these two very different Samoas with a quick return sail to Pago Pago. There we topped off on fuel and water, and did some final mailing and stateside telephoning.

In American Samoa, where almost half of the work

force is on the U.S. Government payroll and many others receive unemployment benefits, apathy abounds, and the "Samoan way of life" seems doomed. In contrast, Western Samoa, proud and independent, though monetarily poor, clings to the traditions and culture of their rich heritage. The people are vibrant, happy, and enthusiastic.

Visiting both Samoas within two short weeks left us saddened by what is happening in American Samoa and by the missed opportunities for growth and development in Western Samoa. With men like Vai Ala'ilima in leadership positions things may change in Western Samoa, but for American Samoa there appears no way out.

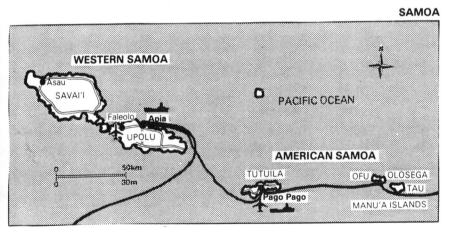

"THE FRIENDLY ISLANDS"—TONGA
(We cross the International Date Line)

THAR SHE BLOWS!! The unmistakable split-tail and huge dark shape of the body told us we had spotted our first whale. Lazily, it spouted vapor ten feet in the air, then gracefully dove along the shoreline at the entrance of the Vava'u Group of islands in Tonga. Our whale refused to pose for pictures as we came closer.

The Kingdom of Tonga, named "The Friendly Islands" by Captain Cook, is a series of almost 200 islands grouped in clusters from north to south along a 600-mile stretch of ocean. It is Polynesia's oldest and last remaining monarchy, and is the only Pacific nation never to have been under foreign rule. We decided to stop briefly in the northern islands of Tonga to break up the 700-mile passage from Samoa to Fiji. We were enchanted, and stayed ten days. One could easily stay a lifetime.

*　　*　　*　　*　　*

We sailed into Neiafu harbor and dropped anchor among boats we had been with before: OCEAN WANDERER from Canada, SINDBAD from Denmark (we had locked through the Panama Canal with them six months earlier), another QUEST II, this one from California, and LA TORTUGA from Spain.

We also met some new boats like the sixty-foot sloop WAR BABY from Bermuda, with it's eleven crew members. It was named TENACIOUS when Ted Turner owned it in the 1970's. In 1989 Warren Brown, the present owner and skipper, won the Cruising Club of America's prestigious Blue Water Sailing Award for sailing WAR BABY to both the Arctic and Antarctic in the same year.

78

We treated ourselves to two nights in the Paradise International Hotel, our first nights off the boat by ourselves in five months. The unlimited hot water, swimming pool, movie theater, and beautiful dining room made it seem quite luxurious. We explored the dusty town of Neiafu and found the Post Office and the Vava'u Handicraft Shop nestled under a huge banyan tree at the town center. The local outdoor market, where we replenished our stores of fruits and vegetables, was just around the corner.

In the Handicraft Shop two friendly women were busy weaving their typically sturdy Tongan baskets by wrapping strips of pandanus leaves around coconut-leaf midribs. They were only too happy to chat with us and pose for pictures.

The traditional Tongan dress includes the *ta'ovala*, a huge woven mat, tied around the mid-section by both men and women as an outer garment. It was quite a sight to see women wrapped in heavy mats from just above their waists to their knees, carrying umbrellas to protect themselves from the heat of the day. A modernized version of the *ta'ovala*, worn by most of the business people we saw, consists simply of a fringed straw belt.

Tonga is one of the four island nations in the South Pacific's "Bible Belt", and on Sundays church and family gatherings fill the day. No stores or restaurants are open and the streets are empty. In Tonga it is even illegal to drive a car on Sunday! But come Monday, people, pigs, chickens, cars and trucks return to fill the dirt streets, and the hum of the town of Neiafu resumes its gentle pace. At our anchorage in the harbor, the sounds of music from the high school band practicing "Edelweiss" greeted us each weekday afternoon.

A New Zealand cruising couple, John and Phyllis Hickey, recently opened The Bounty Bar and Island

Cruising Center in Neiafu. They provide weather and general island information, and serve a delicious breakfast of papaya, pancakes, and coffee on their small deck which overlooks the harbor. We always found the place packed with cruisers, a variety of languages filling the air.

Following the recommendations of the two yacht charter companies in town, Moorings and Rainbow Charter, we took CORMORANT on a five day "cruiser's holiday" to visit some of the more than fifty world class anchorages in the Vava'u Group. These islands are perfect for cruising, and far less crowded than the cruising areas in the Caribbean. In a ten-mile radius of Neiafu there are dozens of small, lush green islands, most of them uninhabited, with white sandy beaches and excellent reefs for snorkeling. Numerous caves carved out of the limestone cliffs by the sea add another dimension to these spectacular mid-ocean islands.

At the tiny island of Tapana we dinghied ashore and hiked five hundred yards along a winding path to the other side for dinner in a thatched hut on the beach, the only structure on the island. The rickety sign over the door boasted, "La Paella Restaurant.... reservations required"! We joined the crews of QUEST II and WAR BABY to fill the place and enjoy an astonishingly authentic five-course Spanish meal. After dinner, we danced on the sand floor to a live three-piece band...the waitress, the chef, and the bartender became the musicians.

Our fiberglass dinghy had suffered major damage while tied to Aggie Grey's cement dock in Apia during some rough weather. We decided Neiafu was the place to get it fixed and went to the only boat yard in town, Don Coleman's. Don is a tall, scraggly-bearded expatriate high school teacher from Oregon who has been in these islands for over eighteen years. His work is excellent and his price was well below what we had anticipated.

South of Samoa the International Dateline makes a jog to the east so that the Kingdom of Tonga is the first country in the world to greet each new day. We learned the phrase: "If it's Sunday in Samoa, it's Monday in the Monarchy" to help us remember. Now, instead of being eight hours behind the East Coast, we were sixteen hours ahead. As we left Tonga, we also left Polynesia and headed towards the island groups of Melanesia. Our next port of call would be Fiji, 500 miles to the west, a major cultural and economic crossroads in the Southwestern Pacific.

THE FIJI ISLANDS....ETHNIC CROSSROADS
(Reefs, Royal Suva Yacht Club, multi-racial people)

The approach to Fiji from the east is fraught with danger. Low-lying islands ringed by coral, and submerged and unmarked reefs scattered like cow pies in a pasture litter the course. Though we had a current chart, the Island Cruising Center in Vava'u had given us a list of twenty-nine uncharted reefs on the way to Fiji that had been sighted by aircraft and commercial vessels.

We had been underway three days before our route took us through the outlying Lau Island Group east of Fiji. We came close along the clearly marked Oneata reef, and at midnight, with the help of our radar and our GPS, passed through this four mile wide gap in the chain of barrier islands. Once we were through the Oneata Passage, Suva, the capital city of Fiji, lay another 200 miles ahead.

We entered Suva Harbor on a bright, brisk morning two days later. Rusting hulks of several fishing vessels lay wrecked on the approaching reefs, reminding us of the lurking hazards for the unwary skipper. Tying to the main wharf of this busy seaport, we awaited the required visit from Customs and Immigration officials.

Hours later, when the five officials finally came on board CORMORANT, the tide was out, and they had to climb down over six feet of cement wall to our decks. As dusk enfolded the city, we finally left the wharf and motored to the back corner of the harbor, anchoring with dozens of other boats in front of the Royal Suva Yacht Club.

Independent since 1972, Fiji still has a distinctly British flavor. In this ethnic crossroads of the South

Pacific, races and cultures mingle with ease. Courtesy and kind words are the order of the day. Suva is spotlessly clean and well maintained, and the buses run on time. The market-place is the biggest and finest in the South Pacific, and clean as a whistle. The post office bustles with gentle efficiency, while across the street international telephone calls are placed in a matter of seconds.

Suva has a large East Indian population. Women in colorful *saris*, the traditional Indian dress, fill the sidewalks, and the scent of curry drifts from Mid-East style restaurants. The many excellent Chinese restaurants offer a tempting alternative. With the favorable exchange rate and reasonable prices, we indulged ourselves.

One day we took a local bus around the island of Viti Levu. For $9.00 each, we had front row seats on a fascinating twelve-hour travelogue. Crossing through the island's interior, our noisy bus bounced and careened along narrow dirt roads. We inched our way across one-lane bridges high above scenic river gorges. Stops at villages and towns every two to three hours afforded welcome rest halts, where we enjoyed sampling the local fare for breakfast and lunch. The last few hours of our trip were on a modern highway from the city of Lautoka back to Suva, past luxury waterfront resorts, to our drop-off at the Royal Suva Yacht Club.

On Sunday we attended Trinity Anglican Cathederal and were warmly welcomed into the multi-racial congregation. Underscoring the Fijian mix of races and cultures, the Dean of the Cathederal is Tongan and his wife English. The pastor is Fijian, and the assistants are from other parts of the South Pacific.

*   *   *   *   *

When we arrived in Fiji we crossed into the Eastern Hemisphere (past the 180 degree longitude), and completed the first full year of our sail around the world. Now, 11,000 miles later, we remain convinced that anything is possible with the Lord's help. We believe that everyone should pursue a dream...like "Happy Talk", the song from *South Pacific*, which keeps running through our minds, says:

> "You've got to have a dream
> If you don't have a dream
> How ya gonna have a dream come true?"

ALONG THE PACIFIC'S RIM OF FIRE IN VANUATU
(Earthquakes, war history, the Blue Hole and Waterfall Bay)

It began as a slight vibration of the floor of the supermarket where Judy was shopping, then the whole building began to rock gently. As canned goods and bottles came tumbling from the shelves, shoppers abandoned their carts and scurried for the safety of the dirt street outside. The town of Luganville was experiencing one of the many earthquakes that occur in this island nation! In a matter of minutes the shopping resumed and the cleanup began, leaving the only two Americans in town just a little shaken up.

*   *   *   *   *

Vanuatu, known as New Hebrides until its independence from the British and French in 1980, is located along the "Pacific rim of fire", where great plates of the earth under the ocean shift frequently, causing much volcanic activity. As CORMORANT entered the island chain early one morning, our first sight was the perfect cone shaped volcanic island of Lopevi, which erupted as recently as 1970, silhouetted against the pink sky.

Before checking in with the authorities in Luganville on the island of Espiritu Santo, we stopped to rest overnight at Vao, which we thought to be a quiet, deserted island. While Ward was still securing the anchor, at least thirty canoes headed our way, filled with friendly children welcoming us to their tiny island. This was to be a common occurrence whenever we anchored near a village.

During World War II there were over 100,000 U.S. servicemen on Espiritu Santo, a support area for the allied offensive at Guadalcanal and the Solomon Islands.

85

A few rusty quonset huts still stand in Luganville, now a sleepy little town, reminders of the former military activity. Peering through the cracks of one quonset hut, we could see metal cots, chairs, and sinks, piled as they had been left by departing American troops nearly fifty years ago. Another was occupied by a family, with chickens scratching in the yard and wash hanging out.

John F. Kennedy and his famous PT-109 were here in 1943, preparing for battle in the Solomon Islands. We walked near the mouth of the Sakarata River where a few fishing boats were tied, trying to picture how it might have looked when the PT boats were there.

A favorite spot for scuba divers is the sunken wreck of the PRESIDENT COOLIDGE, a troop transport ship that struck a "friendly" mine in the harbor and sank close to shore in 1942. Miraculously, all escaped except one man; he is honored by a monument on the shore.

We walked along "Million Dollar Point" where tons of valuable equipment was dumped into the sea by British and American forces at the end of the war. Local plantation owners had refused to purchase the equipment at rock-bottom prices, thinking they could wait and get it free. Smooth-worn coke bottle parts and hunks of rusty, coral encrusted metal now litter the beach.

The official language of Vanuatu is Bislama, a kind of Pidgin English acquired over one hundred years ago when islanders were used as forced labor in Australia. An example of this language is the name of an art store in Luganville: "Art Blong Yu-me", which translates to "Art is for Everyone."

After leaving Luganville we sailed around a point to Palikulo Bay and anchored at "Club Nautique", which turned out to be nothing more than a shelter with picnic tables and an outdoor shower, but a secure spot where cruisers could gather. We washed clothes, took on water, and met some new cruising friends before moving on.

At another stop on Espiritu Santo we took our dinghy up a river to the "Blue Hole", a popular attraction usually reached by taxi. Towards the end of the forty-minute ride we had to push thick watercress aside in the ever-narrowing stream and then, there it was.....a crystal-clear, still, ink-blue pond. Shaded by overhanging trees with gnarled roots reaching from its banks, the "Blue Hole" was over sixty feet deep and forty yards wide. We could clearly see the bottom as we glided across in our dinghy. We enjoyed a swim in the fresh, cool water, and Ward took several swinging jumps from a Tarzan-style rope tied to an overhead branch.

Not far from the "Blue Hole" was a deserted World War II bomber field, a giant clearing in the tall palm trees with occasional patches of pavement peeking through the weeds. A worn path led into the bushes where a small plane lay twisted in a ditch.

CORMORANT sailed further north along Espiritu Santo, and anchored off "Champagne Beach", a picture-perfect crescent of fine sand. At a little-used resort consisting of a few cottages and a small open-air dining room, we enjoyed an excellent lunch of fresh fish. We hiked several miles in the hot sun to the tiny village of Hog Harbor, consisting of one store, a clinic, a church and a school.

Paying a visit to the school, we were introduced to a sixth-grade class, where we sat in on a math lesson and then told the students about our journey. While Bislama is the official language, English is used in all the schools in Vanuatu.

An overnight sail brought us to our final stop in Vanuatu, "Waterfall Bay", on the island of Vanua Lava. About five miles from shore Judy spotted a small dugout canoe adrift. We tied a line to it and towed it into Waterfall Bay. The first person we met there was the owner of the canoe, a young girl named Valery. Her grateful father, Thomas, gave us several pineapples and fresh caught lobsters.

At the end of the day, Thomas and his expectant wife Liza, and most of their nine children: Purity, Hope, Ishmael, David, Valery, Michael, Phillip, Allen and three year old Humility, came on board to watch the video we had taken of them that day. They had all helped us fill our water jugs at the pool created by two giant waterfalls.

The thing we will remember best about Waterfall Bay was the news we received there by radio. Our fifth grandchild, Anne Houston LeHardy, had been born four days earlier in Roanoke, Virginia, to our son, Marcel, and his wife, Nancy. Mother and child were both doing fine!

THE SOLOMON ISLANDS
(Friendly natives, hallowed ground)

Conventional wisdom among the sailing community in the South Pacific is that vessels should head for the shelter of New Zealand or Australia by the 1st of December...the official start of the cyclone season. But Ward had a special date to keep at Guadalcanal on 13 November; so while most boats headed south in late October we sailed north towards the Solomon Islands.

We have reported earlier of being in the shadow of Michener's fabled Bali Hai...at least six islands in the South Pacific claim to be it! As we dropped anchor at Vanikoro, in the Solomon Islands, we read Michener's own words telling us that *this* island was really the source of his inspiration. We were in the center of an ancient volcano, now accessible directly from the ocean through coral reefs and two narrow passes. And there, right in front of us, was *the* "Bali Hai"; green and lush, a spiny ridge and dominating pinnacle reaching for the overcast sky.

Sailing further among the Santa Cruz Islands of the Solomons, we had an overnight sail to Nendo Island, where we officially checked in with Customs. Near the town of Lata, CORMORANT got hung up in a patch of coral for ten minutes before we could free her and anchor in deeper water. Ward dove in to check the damage and found CORMORANT had once again covered for our mistakes...there were only some minor scratches on the keel.

After another sail, this time thirty-six hours due west, we arrived at Santa Anna, a circular, four-mile-wide verdant island. We anchored in the harbor of Port Mary. We had met the daughter of the village chief there two years before in California, so this stop had long been anticipated.

Santa Anna was one of the highlights of our trip. Nestled in the trees at the water's edge was the village of Gupuna. No money is used there; only bartering and trading take place among these contented islanders. Polite, friendly children greeted us.

Every evening at 6 p.m. a loud bell gongs and the two churches (one Anglican, one Evangelical) fill up for brief services of prayers and singing. That was about the only time of day that canoes full of children were not inquisitively circling our boat.

There are two fresh water lakes on this tiny island. We hiked to one of them accompanied by a dozen children, Freda and Alfred in the lead. They were to be our constant companions. One day they guided us up a rough trail to the tiny airstrip where weekly flights linked Santa Anna with Honiara, the capital of the Solomons, located on Guadalcanal.

On the way back to the harbor we waited out a rain storm in a thatched hut used for drying copra, the coconut meat which is the island's main export. As we chewed on some strips of the smoky-tasting copra, a family of pigs scurried out of a rear opening of the otherwise deserted hut.

Reluctantly we left Santa Anna after four days, and sailed along San Cristobal and Malaita Islands and across Indispensable Straits to Ironbottom Sound. During a seven month period of World War II forty-eight ships (Japanese, Australian, and U.S.) were sunk there. More than 19,000 Japanese and 8,000 Americans were killed at Guadalcanal, and it was here that Ward had the rendezvous which had been coming for fifty years. His dad was one of those killed on the bridge of the USS SAN FRANCISCO at two o'clock in the morning on 13 November 1942.

We visited outlying Tulagi Island, home of the US PT Boat fleet during the Solomon Island Campaign, and

Ghavutu Island, where the sea-plane base used to be. With the help of some friendly natives we refilled our water tanks from "the water pump". Not really a pump, this gravity-fed water system, piped from deep within the limestone hills, ends at a spot where ships could anchor and replenish. It still works fifty years after its construction.

Guadalcanal has the highest occurrence of malaria in the world, so we took preventive medication before, during, and after our stay there. We were also careful to return to the boat by late afternoon, when mosquitos were most likely to begin biting.

We stayed in Honiara for one week, anchored near the modern Point Cruz Yacht Club. Enjoying a rare stay in a hotel, we checked into the Japanese-owned Kitana Mendana, to celebrate our thirty-sixth wedding anniversary. On Veterans Day, November 11th, we toured the battlefields with an excellent guide, Michael Ramosaea. "Bloody Ridge", "Edson's Ridge", "Red Beach", the Tenaru River, Alligator Creek, the "Sand Spit" and Henderson Field, all places where U.S. Marines fought so valiantly, were among the stops we made.

Each step was taken softly, for this truly was hallowed ground. It was here that the Japanese were defeated for the first time in ground combat in the Pacific and this, coupled with the US Navy's victories offshore, caused Guadalcanal to become the turning point of World War II in the South Pacific.

On our last day in Honiara we filled CORMORANT with diesel and provisioned for the 1,000-mile sail to Australia. Ward went to the local chart office to get detailed information on Ironbottom Sound. Behind him in line was a Japanese man asking for a map of Bloody Ridge! And anchored beside us was a Japanese sailboat! Fifty years had changed a lot.

Hoisting anchor at 11:00 p.m. under a full moon, we motor-sailed north, then west, following the exact path the USS SAN FRANCISCO had taken fifty years earlier. At 2:00 a.m. we were just south of Savo Island in the middle of Ironbottom Sound, the approximate location where Ward's dad was killed exactly fifty years before.

We stopped the engine, said a prayer for all those brave men who had died there, and tossed a shell lei on the black waters in their memory. After a few minutes we both had the eerie feeling that we were trespassing on sacred seas and didn't want to linger any longer. We started up the engine and headed towards Cape Esperance and the Coral Sea to the south.

SOLOMON ISLANDS

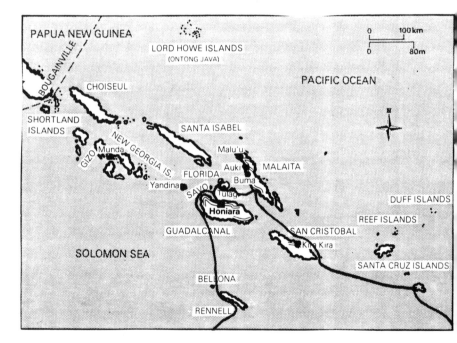

CROSSING THE CORAL SEA, TO AUSTRALIA
(Beset by a storm with 90 mph winds)

Dawn was just peeking over the hills of the western end of Guadalcanal when we turned south and aimed for Australia, on the last leg of our 10,000-mile journey across the Pacific Ocean. On this 1,000-mile stretch we were to experience the worst weather of our entire trip.

We had met cruisers from New Zealand, Tere and Michael Batham, while at anchor in Honiara, and agreed to sail together from Rennell Island to Australia. They were waiting for us on board their forty-six foot steel ketch, SEA QUEST, when we arrived at the southern-most of the Solomon Islands.

Rennell Island, fifty-miles long by ten-miles wide, is the largest raised atoll in the world. The bay where we anchored contained an exceptionally fine coral reef for snorkeling, and here we had our first attempt at night spear fishing. Helpful natives accompanied us, borrowing our waterproof flashlights. We watched in awe while they caught enough lobsters for a huge feast on COR-MORANT that night, the largest lobster measuring three feet from tip to tail!

Traveling with another boat was a new and very agreeable experience for us, with twice-daily radio talks and the comforting sight of their masthead light each night. Ward and Michael had plotted a course to take us to Chesterfield Reef, more than halfway to Australia, and then on to Brisbane.

We left Rennell in good winds, which steadily diminished each day for three days, until there was not a ripple on the water. Clear blue skies and sensational sunrises, sunsets, and starry nights were with us, but where was the wind? Mindful of our limited fuel supply, we were using our engine only when going in and out of harbors and when near reefs. When there was no wind we just drifted, sometimes for hours, patiently waiting.

Finally Chesterfield Reef was close enough to warrant motoring. These remote islands, a possession of France, are made up mostly of underwater reefs. As we carefully approached Isle Longue, one of the few visible islands, hundreds of birds began circling us. Some groups of birds hunting for fish swarmed so thickly that they appeared as small islands on our radar. Ward spotted a humpback whale cavorting in the water, but it disappeared before we could get a closer look.

With SEA QUEST in the lead we entered a pass in the late morning light, the best time of day to spot underwater coral. Michael climbed his mast for a better view as we picked our way through transparent water towards the anchorage. We were using charts with 100-year old information on them, the only ones available.

We anchored in twenty feet of water, so clear that the underwater landscape appeared to be just inches away. Flocks of birds circled overhead while others were gathered along the shoreline of the tiny island, grouped by type of bird, as if by "village".

During our five-day stay at this beautiful, peaceful spot waiting for wind, we explored every inch of Isle Longue and an adjacent reef of sand and coral. Because of the blazing hot sun, we waited until the late afternoon before we dinghied ashore each day. Bird nests were everywhere, in the scrub bushes that stood a little higher than our heads, in the straw-like growth underfoot, and some even underground. An egg or a chick, some quite large and covered with snow-white down, occupied each nest. We were very careful where we stepped! Tere knew all their names....Noddies, Boobies, Petrels, and Great Frigates.

Outside the sandy reef three sharks, one at least ten feet long, grazed slowly by the rock where we stood. In the sand were a confusion of tracks made by giant turtles, each weighing three to four hundred pounds, which came ashore at night to lay their eggs.

When a fresh southeasterly breeze finally blew our way on Thanksgiving morning, we canceled dinner and set sail from our island paradise within the hour. Glad to be underway once again, we were soon disappointed as the winds gradually subsided.

One day we had total calm. We swam, bathed, and practiced our lifesaving operation, with Judy hauling Ward on board in a lifesling using a block and tackle. We set our radar alarm and slept almost all of one night, with no constant watches needed since we were only drifting.

Light winds finally allowed us to use our colorful spinnaker, even leaving it up all night to get 2 to 3 knots of speed out of a tiny breeze. Three days and less than 100 miles out of Chesterfield, we heard an afternoon weather report from Australia that told of a front coming off the Queensland coast headed our way. That should provide steady winds at last.

Building seas and clouds heralded the arrival of the front, and by morning we faced a gray dawn with light rain and 30-knot winds. With a double-reefed mainsail and a handkerchief jib, we were rigged right for those conditions, which stayed with us through the day and night.

The next morning we could see the first signs of blue sky behind the grey storm clouds. But in front of the blue was a darker black cloud with a greenish glow deep within. Lightning, which had been lurking on the horizon, was now striking close to us. The rain increased and pelted CORMORANT horizontally. Ward, dressed head to toe in foul weather gear, came up to relieve a very wet Judy at the wheel.

Within seconds the wind increased to hurricane force...65 to 80 knots, and CORMORANT was slammed down hard on the water, again and again. It was all

Ward could do to hold the wheel hard over, and all Judy could do to brace herself on the cabin floor. The bimini popped out of its stanchions, blocking Ward's vision. All the cushions in the cockpit washed overboard from our nearly horizontal boat.

Inside, Judy watched water come sheeting in along the side walls as she prayed loudly over the din of the wind for the Lord to calm the seas. Things began to float in the cabin as the bilges filled and overflowed, while outside the wind and water combined into a stinging white foam. Visibility was reduced to ten feet in the swirling, slashing water that sounded like a freight train roaring past.

Judy finally was able to open the hatch and ask what she could do to help. " Start the engine!", was Ward's first request; then, "Release the main sheet!". With the mainsail freed, the boat immediately righted itself. Judy joined Ward in the cockpit just as the wind, which had been blowing at hurricane force for half an hour, began to diminish to gale force (35 knots). Lifting the collapsed bimini, we discovered that the forestay had snapped at the top of the mast, and the roller furling system and jib were dragging in the water. Our beautiful spinnaker, which had been bagged and fastened to the lifeline, was gone!

Huge seas crashed around us as Ward moved about the boat checking for damage. The bilges were full and the electric pump had failed. Things were floating on the cabin floor. After Ward lowered and secured the double-reefed mainsail, we set to work bailing the bilges. A hand pump installed in the cockpit took care of the aft bilge under the engine, and we began hauling bucket after bucket from the cabin and the forward bilge.

Tere's voice came up on the radio, reporting that SEA QUEST's mizzen sail had torn but they were otherwise all right. We were only a half-mile apart but still couldn't see each other. We gave them our GPS location and they motored over to find us where we were drifting in the rolling seas. Soon the sky cleared and the sun came out and warmed us all. SEA QUEST waited patiently while we sorted out the jumble of our cabin and made CORMORANT ready to continue on.

Three hours later, bilges bailed, bimini stowed below, and roller furling with attached jib lashed to the side of the boat, we began motoring in broiling hot sun. Ward was able to re-install the bimini the following day, providing us much needed shade.

Without a jib CORMORANT could not point, prohibiting our progress even when light winds came along. And with no forestay we could not trust the mast to support a full mainsail. SEA QUEST, which carried extra fuel, generously offered to transfer several gallons to us at sea. After an elaborate process of floating empty fuel jugs to them and hauling them back onto CORMORANT full, we were on our way. Though forced to motor most of the way, we made some progress under sail by using our storm jib on a spare halyard rigged as a temporary forestay, and using our staysail and double-reefed mainsail.

In the four days that it took us to reach Brisbane we aired wet and salty items from below, thankful for our friends' help and for a God who answers prayers. Never were we so glad to see land as when the coast of Australia came into view!

"CROCODILE DUNDEE" IN REVERSE
(Arrival Down Under; paradise beyond the Pacific)

CORMORANT arrived at the Mooloolaba Yacht Club on the Sunshine Coast of Queensland, Australia on December 11th, exactly one year after heading offshore from Fort Lauderdale, Florida.

A week earlier we had checked in with Australian Customs in Brisbane. Courteous, thorough and competent officials boarded CORMORANT and helped us through the complicated paperwork in record time. They even read through our log book, and brought a dog on board to sniff the boat for drugs! We were soon to learn that friendliness is a way of life in Australia.

The Brisbane River twists and turns its way through the city, narrow enough for the many small ferry boats to cross in less than two minutes. An occasional bridge connects the shores, and tour boats, party boats, and private pleasure boats vie for space on the waterway. We joined in the late afternoon marine traffic as we motored the ten miles upriver to the city center. There we anchored beside SEA QUEST and a dozen other cruising yachts near the beautiful Botanic Gardens. Nearby glistening skyscrapers were a startling sight to us, after our long months in the islands and vastness of the Pacific Ocean.

Strolling through the center of Brisbane we came to the modern Queen Street Mall, all decorated for Christmas and crowded with shoppers. We felt like American "Crocodile Dundees", gaping at the sights. Shiny escalators, exotic toys, fancy clothing on display, brass bands and carolers all caught our rapt attention. We couldn't get enough fresh fruit, salad, pizza, ice cream, or steak. We stayed a week enjoying the wonders of this sparkling city on the edge of the Australian continent.

Soon it was time to say good-bye to SEA QUEST and move on to Mooloolaba, where three months of mail awaited us, and where we had planned to repair and restore CORMORANT after our long sea voyage. Mooloolaba is a popular resort with a beautiful crescent-shaped beach. The Mooloolaba Yacht club, tucked safely away behind a spit of land, offered just what we needed. We planned on a five-month stay, to get our work done and travel around Australia by land, while waiting out the cyclone season.

*   *   *   *   *

Reflecting back on our first year of off-shore sailing, we realized that we had covered over 12,000 miles and visited eighteen different countries and island nations. We spent 130 nights underway at sea, anchored sixty-six times, and found a mooring or tied to a pier the rest of the stops. Day-sailing, where we could anchor at night, brought the total of sailing days to 180, or nearly half the time. In that year we spent only five nights in hotels.

Our longest stay at a dock was at the Pedro Miguel Boat Club in Panama, where CORMORANT was berthed for forty-three days. The longest stretch at sea without sighting land was twenty-two days, crossing from the Galapagos Islands to the French Marquesas. We crossed both the Equator and the International Date Line in this first fascinating year at sea.

Ten different friends, neighbors, and relatives have joined us as crew members for parts of the journey thus far. We've enjoyed all their company and help, especially when Jauncey Sweet helped us on the 5,000-mile stretch from Panama to Tahiti.

We made many new friends both at sea and on land, and learned about other cultures. The geography lessons far surpassed what any book could offer. Speaking of books, Judy read more than fifty, and Ward finally found time to read many that he had been intending to read for years. We learned that we could get along with the very few clothes and other items that fit on the boat, limiting ourselves to the barest necessities. We found that if we had to, the two of us could survive on just a gallon of fresh water a day.

The night sky at sea is a wonder unsurpassed, and the colors of the water near an island and of the coral and fish below the surface are sights to behold. The relatively unhurried pace, except for a few frantic moments, allowed much time for reflection and meditation.

We've been astounded at how much we have in common with other Christians, in spite of the language and cultural differences. We were welcomed when visiting churches in Tahiti, Fiji, the Solomon Islands and Australia. Equally impressive are the cards and letters we receive from a growing network of people who pray daily for our safety.

Besides lessons learned about the boat and sailing we have learned much about ourselves.

JUDY: "I learned that I could handle a frightening situation without panicking. I value every experience we have, whether good or bad, as a learning experience, and am amazed at all I have learned."

WARD: "I've learned that I can be an electrician, a plumber, an engine mechanic, and a sail repairman. When something breaks, and things always do, I've learned how to trace the system to find the cause, and then fix it. And I'm the kind of guy who couldn't change the car's oil before we left on this trip!"

We thank God daily for giving us the opportunity to see the world in this unique way, for allowing us the privilege to meet so many fascinating people, and for the wisdom He provides to help us meet and solve the challenges we face.

Sunset in French Polynesia

Friendly boys come on board in Bora Bora

Tangi-Jimmy, the living legend of Suarrow Atoll

Judy, Vai Ala'ilima and Judy Housley in Western Samoa

Some of our daily visitors at Santa Anna, Solomon Islands

Judy with some of the children of Santa Anna, Solomon Islands

Ward and Michael at Bloody Ridge, Guadalcanal

Some of the thousands of birds at Chesterfield Reef

AUSTRALIA

"Once a jolly swagman camp'd by a billabong
Under the shade of a Coolabah tree,
And he sang as he watched and waited till his billy boiled,
You'll come a Waltzing Matilda with me."

First verse of "Waltzing Matilda"
by A. B. Patterson

POSTCARDS FROM DOWN UNDER
(Cattle, kangaroos and the Snowy River)

In mid-March Cyclone Roger roared down the Queensland coast a hundred miles offshore, spawning forty-foot waves and 100 mph winds, but we were safe and snug in Mooloolaba harbor, waiting for the right time to move north. The cyclone season lasts about four months (December until April) and during that time we repaired CORMORANT and took a month-long land trip throughout southeastern Australia, as far as the island state of Tasmania.

Travelling by train, bus, and ferry boat, we visited Brisbane, Sydney, Orange, Canberra, and Melbourne, and circled Tasmania by car during our eight day stay there. Here are some of our impressions of the wonderful Land of Oz...Australia:

THE PEOPLE:

Friendly, curious, soft-spoken, extremely cordial both to each other and to strangers. They are generous, worldly, and surprisingly reserved. Often we had to initiate the conversation, but once the ice was broken, the Aussies would take over. They love the outdoors and are sports fanatics.

During our thirty-day land trip, we stayed in several Australian homes. Some were sailing friends like Bob and Toni Cruickshank in Sydney, whom we had met in the Marquesas on board QUEST II; others were friends or relatives of people we had met at church in Mooloolaba. On some occasions virtual strangers invited us to their homes; we had two such invitations for Christmas Dinner. And then there was the lady campaigning for Democracy on the steps of the Melbourne Parliament House who invited us to stay at her home.

As we left the cattle ranch of Arthur and Gwenda Ward near the town of Orange (just west of Sydney), Arthur called ahead to his sister, Helen Hunt, at our next stop, Australia's capital city of Canberra. Helen, a writer and artist of considerable talent, met our bus and insisted we stay with her for five days. She then drove us the four hundred miles to Melbourne.

Of the seventeen million people who live in Australia, most live along the coastal areas; the Outback (as the rural, barren center of Australia is called) is lightly populated. About two percent of the population are Aboriginals, native Australians similar to our Native Americans. They are found throughout the land, but predominately in the north and west.

We were in Australia at the time of a national election and became fascinated by the political system. Turned off by the prospect of a goods and services tax (GST) advocated by the favored Liberal Party, the populace voted to keep the Labor Party in power. Hardly any other issues were mentioned in the heated debates that took place as Election Day approached.

Through our church, we became good friends with Owen Davies who was running for the Senate in Queensland. We even helped briefly in his campaign. He lost! It was interesting to us that all Australians are required to vote in national elections. The penalty for not voting is a $50 fine.

Australia's economy over the last hundred years grew on the strength of the sheep's back, with wool being the major industry. Now wool is overproduced and less in demand, resulting in many of the original sheep farming families turning to other products, or selling their land. Australia is caught in the dilemma of being located in the Asian-Pacific region, but with historical and cultural ties to England and America.

Today Australia is at a major crossroads in its history, and no doubt will move more and more into the booming Asian-Pacific marketplace and away from traditional ties to England. Currently, Australia is under the figurehead rule of the Queen of England, but it seems certain that by the year 2000, Australia will be her own Republic. There is even a move underway to change the flag, which now sports the British "Union Jack" in the corner.

THE LAND:

What vast beauty! The train from Brisbane to Sydney took fifteen hours, winding through rolling green countryside reminiscent of the Shenandoah Valley. Sheep and cattle were everywhere, controlled by the wonderful small Welty and Australian Blue cattle dogs which obey the ranchers' arm movements and whistles as they guide the herds.

There are few real mountains in Australia, mostly hills and valleys. In the state of New South Wales we drove to the overlook of the highest peak, Mount Kosciusco, just 7,310 feet high. This is the center of the ski area of Australia. The Blue Mountains, just west of Sydney, offer spectacular canyons, rock formations and waterfalls, and reminded us of the Blue Ridge mountains of Virginia. Were we getting homesick?

For four hours we drove with our new friend Helen Hunt along the winding dirt road that paralleled the Snowy River. This was the location of the very popular Australian movie of 1983, *The Man From Snowy River*, and here was nature at its best. Steep forested hills rose from the river floor, and the river itself twisted and turned along its wide path to the ocean. We saw not one building and only a few people along the way. Often the road left the river's edge to climb winding hills, where we passed through towns consisting of two or three structures, with such irresistible names such as Smiggin Holes and Suggan Buggan.

The ocean coast we travelled was always breathtaking. Picturesque ports, like Coffs Harbor and Lakes Entrance, were packed with fishing trawlers, emphasizing the importance of the sea to this island nation. Commercial fishing and prawning (shrimping) dominate the coastal industry.

It is impossible to describe the vastness that is Australia. On our thirty-day trip we went to four of the six states and one of the two territories, but saw only a fraction of the country.

AUSTRALIA

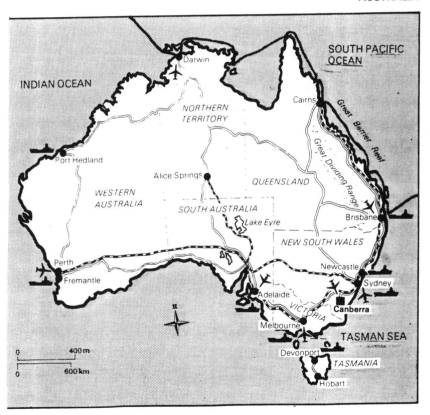

MORE POSTCARDS FROM DOWN UNDER
(Looking over the cities and towns)

SYDNEY:

The premier city of Australia, with one of the finest harbors in the world. The glittering peaked Opera House and the arched Sydney Harbour bridge are classic landmarks here. We climbed to the top of a bridge pylon for a view of the harbor, and later took a ferry boat from Circular Quay to Manly, passing the entrance to the sea. Sydney harbor bustles with shipping, ferry boats, sailboats, fishing boats, and wind-surfers; it reminded us of San Francisco.

We rode to the top of the Sydney Tower, and later shopped in the exquisitely restored Queen Victoria Building. "The Rocks", a warehouse area where Sydney had its beginnings, is now a hodgepodge of shops and restaurants. We were there on St. Patrick's Day, drinking green beer and listening to Irish music as part of a day-long street party.

Over lunch at Mary Reiby's Pub we learned that Mary was typical of the early settlers; having been arrested in 1792 for stealing a horse at age thirteen in England, she was shipped to Australia to serve her seven year sentence. She never left, and ultimately became Australia's first businesswoman.

In Sydney we were also guests in the home of Lee and Hella Sharon. We had met Lee, who was single-handing his sailboat QUEST across the Pacific, on the radio just out of the Galapagos Islands and have maintained contact ever since. He now works on a fishing boat out of Sydney while Hella works at the German Consulate. Lee took us to a park outside of Sydney where we fed and petted kangaroos, koalas, and emus.

CANBERRA:

The Capital of Australia. Sydney or Melbourne would have been the logical choice for the capital of this new country in the early 1900's. Since the people couldn't agree which city to choose, Canberra was built half-way between, in rolling farmland. It was designed to be similar to Washington, D.C., with broad avenues in a majestic circular pattern. We thought it lacked the warmth and character of Australia's other cities.

The Government officially moved here in 1927, and in 1988 the new Parliament Building, with it's soaring, modernistic flagpole was completed. It dominates one side of this circular city, while across the man-made lake sits the imposing War Memorial.

Australia combines tributes to all her military in this one special memorial in Canberra. A morning spent here and we began to appreciate some of the sacrifices Australia made as a young nation. Australia, with a population of only 5 million at the time, lost 61,000 men in World War I, mostly at Gallipoli in Turkey.

Public transportation was lacking in Canberra, but we were able to walk from the Parliament House to the American Embassy, which was built to reflect Williamsburg architecture. We drove to Tidbinbilla Nature Park outside of Canberra where wildlife is in great abundance. Kangaroo bounced up to eat from our hand, and high up in the gum trees, furry koalas lazily chewed on leaves.

MELBOURNE:

We loved this stately city, partly because of its marvelous transportation system, which includes a network of old-fashioned trolley cars. For $2.00 a day, we could hop on any of the many trains, trams, or buses that crisscross the city.

On our first stop in Melbourne we stayed at a Youth

Hostel, a very popular, inexpensive dormitory system (for all ages) throughout Australia. We toured the beautiful Royal Botanic Gardens, the old seaside resort of St. Kilda, and the ancient gaol (jail) where criminals, such as the infamous highwayman Ned Kelley, were hanged.

Touring Victoria's ornate Parliament House, we were impressed with the motto: "Where no counsel is the people fall, but in the multitude of counsellors there is safety".

We went to the magnificently restored old Princess Theater to see "Phantom of the Opera", and heard the Melbourne Symphony Orchestra in the modern, subterranean concert hall. "Moomba", the annual city-wide festival week was ongoing while we were there. Carnivals, ice-carving competition, fireworks, street music, races on the river, and perfect weather made this an enchanting week.

At the Anglican Cathedral (St. Peter's), we heard an excellent sermon that stressed that God is Spirit, not just A spirit; and that God has no body, but is in all bodies of believers.

We had dinner one night at the home of Bill and Lila Brent. Bill, a native of Fredericksburg, was the Chief of the US Information Agency at the Consulate. We also bumped into three old friends; Tom and Mary Ann Nelson, former neighbors at West Point and South Carolina, and Art Bondshu, with whom Ward served in Panama in 1979, proving again what a small world it is.

TASMANIA:

Located 200 miles south of mainland Australia, the island state of Tasmania seems to be about thirty years behind the rest of the country. The seaport capital of Hobart holds the bulk of the population, while the unique charm that is Tasmania is found throughout the countryside. We took a week to circle the island by car, staying at country inns whenever we could.

In Stanley, at the edge of the Bass Strait, we hiked to the top of an enormous volcanic plug, fondly called "The Nut". In Queenstown, in central Tasmania, the earth looks like a moonscape from all the mining and excavations for copper, tin, and zinc.

We strolled Salamanca Place on a quiet Sunday morning in Hobart. This is the scene of a bustling street market on Saturdays. Hoping for a panoramic view of the city, we drove to the top of nearby Mount Wellington, the highest point in Tasmania, where we were met by fog, rain, and howling 40-knot winds. We couldn't see our hands in front of our faces!

We met the famous Tasmanian Devil at Bongorong Park. This black furry animal is the size of a small dog, with strong jaws, sharp teeth, and a piercing screech, renown for its ability to devour animals larger than itself: meat, fur, skin and bones.

Our favorite stretch of Tasmania was the east coast. We constantly seem to be drawn, lemming-like, to the sea, and thus took a fifteen-minute ferryboat ride to Bruny Island. Remote, lightly inhabited, and wild, we rode to what would be the southernmost point on our around the world trip...South Bruny Island...at 43 degrees, 25 minutes south latitude.

At Port Arthur and other prisons in the country, a lot of Australians find their roots. Port Arthur was the penal colony for some of the more serious criminals in this country that was originally settled by convicts. This was home to over 12,500 prisoners for over forty years in the mid-1800's. It is now a beautifully restored site, and probably attracts more visitors than any other location in Tasmania.

We hiked a cliff on Cape Freycinet and overlooked the magnificent azure blue of Wineglass Bay far below...startled by the fact there were no boats at anchor and no people on the three mile white crescent beach. We stopped at the seaside town of Bicheno and

113

hiked to the easternmost point of Tasmania near St. Helens, again lured by the ocean horizon.

In Launceston we went to the spectacular Cataract Gorge, then spent a night in Georgetown, awaiting our return ferryboat ride to mainland Australia. Having traveled to Tasmania on an overnight cruise ship, ABEL TASMAN, we decided to return by the SEA CAT. This huge catamaran carries five hundred passengers and ninety cars, and travels at 40 knots. In four hours we zipped across the treacherous Bass Strait, then returned to Melbourne by bus.

MOOLOOLABA/MAROOCHYDORE:

This seaside resort area fifty miles north of Brisbane has been our home base for four months. If we weren't Americans, we would want to be Australians and live in Mooloolaba. Mooloolaba is an Aboriginal word meaning "where the waters meet". It was here that we felt right at home, thanks to St. Peter's/St. Elizabeth's Church, which we joined, and the Returning Service League (RSL), an organization of ex-servicemen.

Del and Heather Douglas and David and Brigitte Ward of the church made us part of their families. Mike Gunn of the RSL even came down to the boat yard to help us sand and paint CORMORANT's bottom for two days. When the job was finished, Joyce Gunn fed us all a typical Australian "barbie" at the nearby ocean-front public barbecue grill.

We also spent time with Arthur and Val Pearson. Arthur, approaching his eightieth birthday, regaled us with tales of the Australian Army in World War II, where he was present for the first shot fired (North Africa in 1940), and the last shot fired (New Guinea in 1945). He also saw combat action in Syria, Greece, Ceylon and Indonesia in between.

The beach at Mooloolaba is a gorgeous crescent of white sand and surf. It is in constant motion with surf-

114

ers, outrigger canoe races or the mighty Australian Surf Boat races, but with room for quiet sunbathing as well.

When we left Mooloolaba to sail north along the Great Barrier Reef, we realized how much we would miss all of our friends there. We won't ever forget them or that special place.

With crusing friends atop "Cook's Look", Lizard Island, Australia

CRUISING THE CORAL COAST
(From Mooloolaba to Middle Percy Island)

When Captain James Cook sailed up this coast in 1770, he was mystified by the relatively calm waters. Later he discovered that off the entire northeastern coast of Australia, stretching over more than 1200 miles, was a barrier reef, blocking much of the Pacific Ocean swell.

A series of coral-reef islands, mostly underwater, this wonder of nature lies about 200 miles offshore at the southern end, and comes close to the coast at the northern end. The Great Barrier Reef is fifty miles wide in places, and since it is alive and growing, it harbors a myriad of colorful and interesting varieties of sea life. Research shows it to be between two and eighteen million years old, and it is the largest living thing in the world. Captain Cook charted most of the area after discovering it, and found some of the passes where ships can enter the reef from the open ocean.

Between the reef and the mainland lie dozens of continental islands, most of them uninhabited. Some are formed of sand and others, having once been connected to the mainland, show high, rocky peaks. Foliage and wildlife are abundant, and protective bays exist throughout the islands. It was in these popular and dramatic cruising grounds that we were to spend the next several weeks.

* * * * *

Waving good-bye to Australian friends, we glided COR-MORANT out of her slip at the Mooloolaba Yacht Club. In the four months we had been there, we had repaired our sails, our forestay and roller-furling, and our engine. CORMORANT had spent the last week in

116

Mooloolaba out of the water for rudder repair, scraping and sanding, and a new coat of anti-fouling bottom paint. We were now ready and anxious to get back to sea.

On board with us were Helen Hunt and Caroline Clevenger. Helen, our artist friend from Canberra, wanted a taste of ocean sailing, and Judy's young cousin, Caroline, was on a six month backpacking trip in Australia. Both sailed with us for four days to Bundaberg, the closest port city to the north.

Ahead of us lay some of the most enjoyable sailing in the world; inside the Great Barrier Reef of Australia. From Mooloolaba we sailed one night in open waters under windy and rolly conditions. It was a night Helen would like to forget! At dawn's high tide we negotiated the tricky sand bar connecting Fraser Island to the mainland and found the calm waters of the Great Sandy Strait.

A robust sail across Hervey Bay brought us to the mouth of the Burnett River. We followed the river for ten miles to Bundaberg, in the middle of the sugar-cane growing area. Bundaberg claims to be where the Great Barrier Reef begins, but it is more renown in Australia as the home of the famous Bundaberg Rum. We enjoyed a tour of the distillery.

ANZAC Day, standing for Australian New Zealand Army Corps Day, occurred while we were in Bundaberg. The whole town turned out for the parade along wide, tree-lined streets. A smartly dressed bagpipe band led the way, followed by elderly war veterans, some walking and some riding in jeeps. Boy Scouts, Girl Guides, more bands and military organizations marched by. Each group laid a flower wreath at the war memorial in the town square.

Helen and Caroline bid us good-bye at the quaint Bundaberg train station. Soon we set sail, back down the river and a twenty-eight hour sail up the coast. Squally conditions forced us to seek shelter in Island Head Creek, along the mainland, where we waited for better weather.

A glorious sail with the prevailing southeast wind behind us brought us in one day from our place of refuge to the Percy Isles. We chose to anchor at the largest of these, Middle Percy. We had heard of its sole permanent inhabitant, Andy Martin, and wanted to meet him.

An artist named Bev was the first person we encountered ashore. She lives in a tree house near the beach for several months each year, painting colorful island impressions. She showed us through her unusual dwelling, reached by circular steps around a tree trunk, and then pointed the way to the trail to "The Homestead".

The only real house on the island, The Homestead is at the summit, a two-mile hike up a jungle path from the small bay where we had anchored. Andy, an Englishman who has lived there for more than thirty years, was one of the most interesting characters we would meet.

A tall, lean man, he appeared to be in his late sixties, and was eager to stop what he was doing to have a chat over a glass of fresh limeade. We covered every subject from politics to religion, his special interest being a book he is writing expounding on a Biblical theory of his.

A young family with two small children had recently moved to the island. They helped care for Andy's many animals and tended his extensive vegetable and herb garden. John, the husband and father, is building a stone house nearby and makes occasional runs to the mainland for supplies in his old sailing "lugger", a type of boat formerly used for pearling. Liz and the two small boys, Jacob and Joshua, work in the garden. She prepared a delicious lunch of fresh salad and homemade bread, cheese, honey, and lemon-grass tea, as she does for any visiting yachters who make the trek to The Homestead.

At lunch we sat with Andy and all the family around a rustic wooden table on the open-air porch. Five year old Jacob impressed us with his knowledge, from Bible stories to the welding of boat parts. Peacocks, chickens, goats, geese, and dogs roamed the yard, gathering beneath the open windows for scraps they knew would be tossed down to them at mealtimes. Several horses were allowed to run wild, showing up now and then for food. In an enclosure in the open area under the house were eight golden lab puppies, who swarmed around Andy when he brought them milk and a goat's leg for lunch.

Loaded down with bananas, fresh greens, and herbs that we purchased from Liz, we headed back down the path. Near the shore was a large lean-to shelter, to which had been affixed hand painted planks bearing the names of boats that had visited the island over a period of nearly twenty years. We hammered up a small CORMORANT plank to add to the jungle of signs.

The following day we set sail before dawn, with over sixty miles to go before dark. As Middle Percy Island faded in the distance, we realized how fortunate we were to have visited that unique spot and the fascinating people who call it home.

Andy Martin at "The Homestead" atop Middle Percy Island

THE QUEENSLAND COAST
(Island-hopping along northeastern Australia's coast)

The Whitsunday Islands off the Queensland Coast are one of the most popular attractions in Australia. Arthur and Gwenda Ward, whom we had visited on their cattle farm in New South Wales, had never seen these islands, so they accepted our invitation to sail with us in the Whitsundays for a week.

Just an afternoon's sail from the coastal resort town of Airlie Beach, this group of seventy-four spectacular rock-peaked islands are a beacon for charter boats and cruisers like ourselves passing through. Captain James Cook named the islands in honor of the day he discovered them, Whit Sunday, in 1770, then later realized that he hadn't taken into account the International Date Line! The name stuck just the same.

Each day we anchored at a different spot: fiord-like Nara Inlet on Hook Island, a protective bay on Border Island, a rather rolly bay on Haslewood Island where we reef-walked at low tide among large clams encased by coral, and in the protective lee of Whitsunday Island, near the exclusive resort island of Hamilton. There we dinghied ashore for an ice cream cone and a ride around the island in a rented golf cart for some thrilling views. Most of the clientele at this prestigious resort were Japanese honeymoon couples!

One day we anchored off the famous and beautiful Whitehaven Beach on Whitsunday Island, taking a picnic lunch ashore. Five miles of powdery white sand gives the beach its name.

On our final day with Arthur and Gwenda on board, we sailed up the delightful Whitsunday Passage, the wind behind us as we glided past more of the islands, some uninhabited and some with attractive resorts. Back at

Airlie Beach the bustle of the marina contrasted sharply to our quiet days among the islands.

*   *   *   *   *

Alone and continuing our way northwest up the Queensland coast, we anchored each night in a protected spot. One anchorage was behind Cape Upstart, so named by Captain Cook, who had been startled at the sudden appearance of its high cliffs.

One rainy night we anchored behind the low sand islet of Cape Bowling Green among five fishing trawlers, rolling unpleasantly in the choppy sea swell and a brisk 25-knot breeze. We maintained an anchor watch that night.

Deciding to skip Townsville, the largest city along Australia's tropical coast, we instead visited nearby Magnetic Island. There we dropped our hook in picture-perfect Horseshoe Bay. We rode a local bus that wound its way past rocky precipices overlooking inaccessible bays to a small community where boats arrived constantly, bringing visitors from Townsville. Backpackers were especially welcome on Magnetic Island, and we liked the informal atmosphere.

We used the beach-side telephone booth at Horseshoe Bay to call Linda and Jauncey Sweet in Fredericksburg. Linda, who forwards our mail, told us to expect three packs of letters when we reached Cairns, our next port.

Spectacular Hinchinbrook Channel separates the soaring mountains of Hinchinbrook Island from the nearby mainland. After a rather ignominious start in the channel when we briefly went aground on a sand bar as the tide was going out, we motored for several hours through the tropical greenery of the curving waterway.

Carefully we followed leads and range markers to stay

inside the channel, and anchored in a small creek deep within the passage. There we rested for two days in calm water among the quiet mangroves in the shadow of the towering mountain peaks.

Still on Hinchinbrook but out of the passage and around to the east is one of the most intriguing places we have yet discovered. We anchored near Cape Richards and went ashore in our dinghy to see a resort we had read about.

Named "Splendid Isolation", the resort caters to fewer than thirty guests, offering individual cottages in the woods, hiking trails, and an elegant but casual dining room in the open air, nestled among palm trees and other rich tropical growth. A private beach and pool was available, and the sunsets were free!

We treated ourselves to a gourmet lunch at the resort and learned that Hinchinbrook is the largest island in the world that is entirely a national park. Boats deliver backpackers to remote camping and hiking spots, as well as guests to the resort.

On a rocky overlook with a view of the entire bay, parrots flashed their green, red, and blue feathers above us, and an occasional three-hundred pound turtle swam by 100 feet below. There we watched another spectacular sunset along the Great Barrier Reef.

Perhaps it was the scuzzy day we picked to arrive at Dunk Island, or the following rainy day which kept us boat-bound, but whatever the reason, we were disappointed by this popular island. Tourists arrive regularly by plane or the frequent boat service from the mainland to enjoy the beautiful and expensive resorts, but there were no facilities for "cruisers" like us. During our brief time ashore we were impressed with the dense jungle growth, and enjoyed hiking over an authentic swinging bridge that spanned a deep gorge.

The bustling river town of Cairns (pronounced "Cans") is the unofficial capital of northern Queensland,

and a mecca for cruisers. We moored fore and aft to pilings on the far side of the river, along with a hundred other boats, and dinghied across the river to the Cairns Yacht Club, now dwarfed by high-rise neighboring hotels.

The fast-growing tourist industry has caused many changes, yet Cairns seems to retain at least some of its rustic ambiance. The international airport provides easy access to the Great Barrier Reef for Australia's many visitors. We met Americans from Georgia, South Carolina, and North Carolina, but Japanese are the main tourists, and over seventy-five percent of them are honeymooners.

In Cairns we saw two movies, ate ice cream and pizza, and had a few "pots" of beer with sailing friends at the Yacht Club. We also rented a car for a day to see some of the inland sights. A walk through the Rain Forest Habitat near Port Douglas gave us another closeup view of kangaroos, koalas, colorful butterflies and parrots, and, for the first time, bats. With a two-foot wing span and a great swishing sound, one bat definitely got our attention as he swooped out of the trees and landed on our guide's arm. A tame creature, he loved to have his stomach scratched!

We also watched bungy-jumping for the first time. From a 300-foot platform, jumpers leaped head first with their feet tied to a strong elastic cord. They are jerked half-way back up in the sudden bounce at the end of the tether. Definitely an event for the younger generation!

Up in the hills behind Cairns we stopped at the picturesque village of Kuranda, and saw the impressive, gaping gorge at Barron Falls. We also hiked across the swing bridge at the scenic Mossman Gorge further to the north.

We added to our provisions on each dinghy trip to town, and after ten relaxing days set sail for Cape York, the northern tip of Australia. Cairns would be the last modern city until we went "over the top", through the formidable Torres Straits and on to Darwin, 1,400 miles away.

With PING and CORMORANT on Whitehaven Beach in the Whitsunday Is.

ALONG AUSTRALIA'S GREAT BARRIER REEF
(We round the continent's northern tip)

The history of this stretch of Australia's waters, along the continent's northeast coast, is riveting. Here Captain James Cook's journey almost ended in disaster.

Just before midnight on June 10, 1770, at the mid-point of the first of Cook's three famous voyages, the agonizing sound of wood crunching on coral brought the entire crew topside. Cook had just "discovered" the Great Barrier Reef, as the three-masted, square-rigged, 180-foot ENDEAVOR found itself stuck on an underwater reef. On our trip, CORMORANT sailed safely past that spot, now clearly marked on all charts as Endeavor Reef, and on to Cooktown, fifty miles to the north.

This frontier-style town was established on the banks of a river where ENDEAVOR finally came to shore for six weeks of repairs after twenty-three anxious hours on the reef. We were there for the 223rd anniversary of that landing, and we found Cooktown alive with a festive atmosphere.

The carnival weekend was pure Australian, with all of ten horses in the grand parade, a tug of war, wet tee-shirt contests, auctions, dancing, beer flowing as freely as water, and games for the kids.

At the top of Grassy Hill, we stood where Cook had looked seaward, plotting his course to escape the confines of the reef. We also toured the Cook Museum, which now possesses portions of Cook's logbook and the huge anchor ENDEAVOR left on the reef. It was recovered in 1971.

For the first time in our travels we saw large numbers of Aborigines. Here on the Cape York Peninsula, isolated Aboriginal settlements are among the few populated areas.

The three pubs in Cooktown did an overflow business during the weekend, and ear-splitting rock 'n roll music caused us to leave sooner than planned. We left in the dim light of pre-dawn to take full advantage of the high tide, crossing the shallow sandbars of the Endeavor River.

Still following Cook's path, we used our new colorful sail, a blue and white modified spinnaker, to pull us along the fifty miles to Lizard Island. This is the island that is closest to the outer edge of the Great Barrier Reef.

As we arrived, our New Zealand friends, Brian, Louise, and their son, Hedley, on ASTRON, told us of their catch that day: an eight-foot marlin. We went over to their boat to celebrate and left with delicious marlin steaks to cook for dinner.

With sailing friends from the boats FIDDLER, ASTRON, and GOLDEN APPLE of the SUN, we hiked ninety minutes to Cook's Look, at the top of Lizard Island. From here Cook discovered Cook's Pass, through which he later sailed to the open ocean, finally free of the reef.

We put out a second anchor as the wind increased, gusting to more than 40 knots, and rain squalls battered our now-crowded anchorage. Boats continued to arrive, most of which we had been with at one point or another during our trip up the Great Barrier Reef. We had met WIRRAWAY and ROAMA, both Australian boats, on Hope Island, just before Cooktown; INTEGRITY had been beside us at Dunk Island, and several Scandinavian boats, KOLORIT, MORNING SUN, ZEVALK, and CARLISA, had been with us at Mooloolaba.

More than twenty-eight boats gathered during the five days we spent at Lizard Island, escaping the rolling seas brought by this sudden spell of bad weather. Now the hazard wasn't coral or rocks, but other boats dragging their anchors.

Snorkeling during one of the few sunny days at Lizard, we explored an underwater cliff of coral just fifty feet from our boat. Fish of all sizes and hues swam among the graceful and colorful coral branches. Giant clams, with gaping four-foot wide velvety-lined mouths, were encrusted in the jagged reef below us. In this protected anchorage we also saw a huge turtle, and at a distance a few 250-pound "potato cod" fish.

Ashore were a private resort, a small airstrip, and the Lizard Island Research Station, where scientific study of the Great Barrier Reef is conducted. We were surprised to learn just how delicate a balance exists between all the elements that keep a coral reef healthy and growing.

Along the beach were the remains of Mrs. Watson's stone house. Mrs. Watson, a local resident, escaped from attacking Aborigines in 1880 by going to sea in a large cooking vat with her baby and a Chinese cook, her husband being away on an extended fishing trip. She landed forty miles downwind on a deserted island, only to die of thirst. She recorded their trials in a diary now on display, along with the cooking vat, in the Brisbane Museum.

For eight of the next ten days after leaving Lizard Island we saw no living souls except fellow sailors and some pearl farmers, even though we anchored each night at picturesque islands or in sheltered coves on the mainland.

There is only one small fishing village, Portland Roads, along this three hundred mile stretch of the Australian coastline. The isolation and rough dirt roads make the Cape York Peninsula ideal for backpackers and four-wheel-drive vehicles.

Heading "over the top" of Australia, the sailing conditions were the best we had experienced since the Solomon Islands. Each day, we would hoist anchor at dawn and sail downwind with a poled-out jib, "wing-and-wing" with the mainsail, in brisk 25-knot winds.

Two experienced yacht racers, Australian Jack Williams on WIRRAWAY and New Zealander Phil Atkinson on GOLDEN APPLE, had shown us how easy it was to handle our heavy pole, which we had hesitated to use before. We traveled in a small "fleet" with those two boats and others for almost a month.

At one anchorage, in Owen Channel of the Flinders Group of islands, we all agreed to stay an extra day. We dinghied across the channel to Stanley Island, where in caves high up a hill we found Aboriginal rock paintings. Hundreds of years old, these paintings depicted local animals and people, and a few showed sailing vessels of the period of European exploration.

One day thirteen year old Hedley, from ASTRON, sailed with us. We were delighted to have this helpful and nimble youth along. He is continuing his education at sea using a correspondence course from New Zealand, while they motor around the world in their sixty-foot trawler, designed and built by Hedley's father, Brian.

As we approached Cape Grenville, the Australian Coast Watch plane flew over our entire fleet. We now numbered about twenty boats, and stretched over ten miles. Coast Watch called each boat on the radio for identification, as they kept track on all vessels in these remote areas, looking for illegal immigrants.

Leaving an anchorage in the deserted Escape River, we eased over the shoal on a rising tide and headed north. Three hours later we entered Albany Passage, a four mile long, narrow and swift channel between the mainland and Albany Island. Once past the entrance shoals and reefs we felt like we were on a conveyor belt, the current carrying us along at 10 knots while the scenery of green foliage, red and brown cliffs, huge red dirt ant hills, and sparkling white beaches whizzed past us.

A week behind us at Albany Passage, CARLISA was lost when Carl, a seventy-two year old single-hander from Sweden, misjudged the entrance reef and ran aground.

He was pulled to safety by a Coast Watch helicopter but his boat was destroyed in the relentless crush of waves on coral.

Once through Albany Passage we elected to sail directly in front of the tip of Cape York, coming through a short, deep, narrow passage within twenty yards of the northern point of continental Australia. With sails up and motor idling as a precaution, we rounded the tip and then dropped anchor a half mile to the west, in the lee of Cape York.

Our two month, 1,700-mile passage up the Great Barrier Reef was behind us and we both felt a satisfying sense of relief and accomplishment.

"OVER THE TOP" TO DARWIN
(In an isolated spot, cruisers rally around CORMORANT)

CORMORANT was the first in our "fleet" of seven boats to drop anchor in quiet Simpson's Bay, five miles west of Cape York on the northeastern tip of Australia. It was here, away from all civilization, that our BMW engine decided to quit! We have learned to anticipate things breaking on our boat, but not such a critical item so far from help.

We normally use the engine to set the anchor by backing down on it, and also to free the anchor by going forward. Now we were faced with a 350-mile stretch of open sea across the Gulf of Carpentaria to the small port of Gove without an engine. We would need plenty of wind to keep up with the others, once we managed somehow to get underway.

One by one other boats arrived at Simpson's Bay and soon four friends came on board to help Ward "troubleshoot" the problem. John Ivey, an Australian from KEKENI turned out to be a diesel mechanic by occupation and soon pinpointed a faulty oil pump.

A radio call by Phil on GOLDEN APPLE to a supplier he knew in Brisbane soon had a new BMW oil pump located and on the way by air to Gove. After a weekend's rest for all seven boats, Kit and Richard Curtis, Americans from FIDDLER, helped us free the anchor by powering CORMORANT forward with their strong dinghy engine. ASTRON towed us out past nearby rocky islands to the open waters, and turned us into the wind so we could hoist our sails.

Strong winds and often lumpy and uncomfortable seas were with us for the two-and-a-half-day sail across the Gulf of Carpentaria, and our wind generator kept our batteries fully charged. At Gove, we were the only boat to sail all the way in, tacking back and forth in the narrow channel and successfully dropping anchor and sails among the fifty other boats at the Gove Yacht Club, something we had never tried before.

The new oil pump arrived by air at the tiny nearby town of Nuhlumbuy and, thanks to John on KEKENI, our engine was soon running. Again we were struck by the way cruisers come to each other's aid, and with combined talents can solve most challenges.

The annual "Over the Top Rally" of thirty boats soon left Gove for Darwin, a 500-mile stretch to be covered in ten days, with anchorages planned nearly every night. Ironically the wind died as we started, but now that we had a functioning motor we could keep up with the fleet. It was a spectacular scene when all thirty boats lined up to pass in single file through the dramatic "Hole in the Wall", a deep, fifty-yard wide opening between two barrier islands, a shortcut saving over thirty miles.

Beach barbecues, fishing contests, and other activities took place at each stop, making for a fun-filled trip. We and our Danish friends, Ruth and Bent on KOLORIT, both had reasons for pressing on towards Darwin, however, so we left the fleet at the "Hole in the Wall" anchorage and struck out together for the remaining 400 miles.

One night we anchored in the lee of Cape Don, the last good protection until Darwin. At dawn we motored in total calm, but anticipating strong winds once we cleared the protection of the land, we put a double reef in our mainsail. Sure enough, as we eased our bow around Cape Don, 30-knot winds hit us on the nose. Rollicking seas stayed with us until the tide changed in our favor, giving us a pleasant ride on milky-jade waters for the remaining hundred miles to Darwin.

*   *   *   *   *

Darwin is a frontier town that has modernized. With

131

wide streets, a prompt bus system, an international airport, and pervaded by an edge-of-the-continent mentality, Darwin is a delightfully unique city.

87,000 people live in Darwin, where the annual average beer consumption is twenty-four gallons per man, woman, and child, the highest in Australia. Huge crocodiles live in the estuaries of Darwin. While on a small tour boat up the Adelaide River we saw these wild mammals leap out of the water their full length when offered meat at the end of a long pole.

At Darwin we came alongside a pier on the high tide of a twenty-four foot tidal change, to have CORMORANT lifted out of the water and stored for two months. We had always planned to take a lengthy break from our trip at this point, and returned to the U.S. for ten weeks to see our family, meet ten-month old Anne Houston LeHardy for the first time, and celebrate our son, Ward, Jr.'s marriage to Debbie Smith of Houston, Texas.

*   *   *   *   *

Two years had brought a lot of changes to Fredericksburg. There were significantly more people, cars, and businesses than we remembered, and new roads and buildings were everywhere. The commuter rail was finally running! A sparkling new hospital opened while we were in town. We listened to Rush Limbaugh for the first time and found him to be right on target on most issues.

We enjoyed the best of both of the worlds we live in. Seeing friends and family in Hawaii, and from New York to South Carolina, was wonderful. It was also exciting knowing that the sailing lifestyle we enjoy so much lay just a few weeks away when we would return to Darwin and continue our trip around the world.

Sydney Bridge viewed from atop a pylon

Brian and Louise Pearce and their 8' marlin at Lizard Island

SOUTHEAST ASIA

On the road to Mandalay,
Where the flyin'-fishes play,
And the dawn comes up like thunder
Out of China 'crost the Bay!

From: "Mandalay"
by Rudyard Kipling

FROM DARWIN TO BALI:
(Culture shock: a taste of the Spice Islands)

We were a hundred miles into our five day sail across the Timor Sea from Darwin, Australia to Indonesia, when it seemed we had a potential disaster on our hands. Ward had just looked into the engine room and discovered a major oil leak; about four quarts lay under the engine in a puddle and more was streaming out.

Fortunately, CORMORANT was in glassy-calm seas, allowing conditions for Ward to clean up the mess and then pinpoint the problem, a dried-out gasket. He tightened the three nuts which hold the two parts together, and applied a quick-dry, metal-hard epoxy around the gasket. We waited the recommended three hours, then, with our hearts in our throats, started the engine. Praise God, no leaks! We continued on to Kupang, three hundred miles away, with no further incident except for a whole day spent by Ward repairing the "head" (toilet).

These were typical of the challenges we face, especially after leaving the boat out of the water for two months in the blistering heat and dry conditions of Darwin. Having just returned from our two-month break in the U.S., we were now in a hurry to stay ahead of the monsoon season, due to begin in five weeks.

In Kupang we would meet our Navy son, Peter, and his fiancee, Carla Sibson. They were to join us for a short vacation week in between his change of assignments from Hawaii to Florida.

*   *   *   *   *

Kupang! This small, crowded city offered a stark contrast to the orderliness and cleanliness of Darwin. It

136

was a fascinating introduction to Indonesia, the former Dutch East Indies; the "Spice Islands" of sea lore.

Located on the southwestern corner of the island of Timor, Kupang is the capital of this once divided island. The Dutch owned the western half until Indonesia gained independence in 1949. The Portuguese continued to own the eastern half of the island until as late as 1975, when Indonesia seized it by force in a brutal invasion. Tensions remain high in East Timor, where many still seek independence from Indonesia, but we were completely safe in Kupang.

Viewed from the sea, an uneven skyline of old cement structures seems to grow right out of the rocky shoreline. The city came alive in the pre-dawn light, first with the haunting chant of Muslim prayers, then the honking of horns mingled with the sound of boat engines. Soon brightly painted boats scurried past us in all directions.

We had anchored near the center of town, right by Teddy's Bar, where sailing friends had told us to ask for Jimmy. Teddy's, located right on the trash-strewn beach where we landed our dinghy, was packed with Australians. We soon found friendly Jimmy Rahman, a wiry, enthusiastic Indonesian who makes a living helping foreign boats check in through the maze of bureaucracy that is official Indonesia.

In our case that involved half a day tied up to a fishing boat at the customs pier. Ten officials came on board, each wanting a coke, a beer, or money. Jimmy advised us to be calm and just endure the process. Later, Jimmy rode out to us standing on the deck of a rickety wooden boat to deliver fuel by hand pump from a fifty-five gallon drum. The boat owner's entire family came along just to see the Americans!

Later we hopped on a "bemo", (a gaudily decorated ten-passenger mini-bus blaring rock and roll music) and went careening through the narrow, twisting streets with

Jimmy's cousin, Linda Karstan, who had offered to show us around. In the local museum we saw artifacts representing the rich culture of the area, as well as charts showing where the Japanese had come ashore during World War II.

Linda took us to her house for lunch and a "shower", which consisted of two tubs of cold water, a large plastic one and a fixed one, and a plastic scoop. Water drained from the cement floor to the open sewer, which lines all the streets of Kupang. With our limited water supply on the boat we were grateful for this opportunity! Linda was an able guide and companion, and even took Judy to the beachside market the morning we left.

We met Peter and Carla at Kupang's dusty, hilltop airport and later that night enjoyed a delicious Indonesian dinner at a tiny, open air restaurant. The bill for six of us (Jimmy and Linda had joined us) came to the equivalent of $12.00; one of the reasons Australians flock here for vacations.

With Peter and Carla on board, we set off at dawn for a thirty-six hour sail to the north coast of Flores Island. We knew we would see plenty of fishing and boat traffic along the way, but we never imagined the magnitude of it all.

Each island in Indonesia seems to have its unique type of fishing boat, or "prahu", and its special way of catching fish. Just outside Kupang Harbor dozens of enormous boats, each moored permanently, were rigged with a huge array of netting. At night these nets are lowered, and bright lights are used to attract fish. Literally tons of fish are gathered in each night by these fifty or so vessels, which look like a small city when viewed from the shore at night.

We day-sailed along the north coast of Flores Island, anchoring among fish traps and fishing boats each night. Hundreds of "prahus" with their bright green or blue sails glided along the waters off each village. At a deserted island near the fishing village of Labuhan Bajo, we snorkeled as wild monkeys watched from the thick foliage behind the beach.

After seeing Peter and Carla off at the tiny airstrip of Labuhan Bajo, we decided to sail the twenty miles to Rindja Island, even though it was late in the day. We like to change locations as a way of perking our spirits up when our children leave us.

We had been given the location of an anchorage recommended by others, but the coordinates proved to be incorrect by about a mile. As a result, we mistakenly sailed into the midst of a pearl farm and got chased away by a boat load of gun-toting security men just at dusk. We were forced to motor several miles back in the fading light. Rounding a point aimed at the correct anchorage, but without enough time to get there before dark, we had no choice but to anchor in the first suitable depth, now in the pitch black.

At dawn we awoke to find the tide low and CORMORANT surrounded on three sides by coral, but with plenty of room to swing on our anchor, which was set in forty feet of water. We thanked the Lord and our accurate depth sounder and radar, which helped us find that spot after dark.

We continued on to the right anchorage; a perfect, circular bay a mile wide and thirty feet deep. Ashore at the Ranger station of a National Park, a guide, David, led us on a two hour hike. We spotted dozens of jabbering monkeys, deer, birds, and finally the animal we really came to see; the renowned Komodo Dragon. One of these giant lizards, at least six feet long, weighing over a hundred pounds, was sleeping on a hilltop beside a log overlooking the bay and CORMORANT. These monsters can devour an entire deer, then sleep for a week.

An overnight sail past towering volcanic islands brought us to Lombok Island, where we spent a day at anchor, snorkeling, changing the engine oil, and generally preparing for three crew members who would join us for a few weeks at our next stop, the fabled island of Bali.

Indonesian fishing boat off the Java Coast

BALI
(Colorful island draws tourists like a magnet)

The delightful island of Bali sits like a tiny jewel midway along the Indonesian archipelago, which stretches over more than three thousand miles, as far as the distance from New York to California. About twice the size of the state of Rhode Island, Bali attracts tourists like a magnet.

Arriving at the small but busy port of Benoa, near the international airport and Denpasar, the capital, we were assisted by cheerful Made Gerip, of Bali Yacht Services. He appeared alongside CORMORANT in his motor boat as we entered the harbor, and led us to a mooring, then arranged to complete our complicated check-in procedures with the authorities. He helped us take on fuel and water, and even took our laundry. Indonesia was the first country we visited where little English is spoken, so we were especially grateful for Bali Yacht Services.

We remained at Benoa, a long dinghy ride from shore and a half hour bus ride from the city and airport, just long enough to meet our arriving crew, nephew Schuyler Sweet from Fredericksburg, and Charlie and Pat Poole from Fort Lauderdale, FL. The Pooles would remain on board for two weeks, and Schuyler would go on to Malaysia with us.

Denpasar swarmed with cars and motorcycles and the ever present "bemos", which we used to get into town for about twenty-five cents. There are almost no crosswalks or traffic lights, and few sidewalks in this capital city, which bustles with hordes of people.

Once our crew had assembled we all decided to explore inland Bali for a few days. We headed to the quiet town of Ubud, a cultural center nestled in the cooler climes of Bali's foothills. There we stayed at Oka Kartini's Bungalows, which are patterned after an old palace courtyard. Elaborately carved gilded doors, richly carved furniture, colorful statues, velvet covers, and fresh cut flowers placed throughout, blended in tasteful simplicity. The perfect climate allowed most of the rooms to be in the open air.

From Ubud we took a day trip by car to visit elaborate Hindu temples, ancient ruins, volcanoes, and a wood carving shop. Our road passed through tiny villages and wound past rice fields symmetrically cut into the steep hillsides.

We visited Goa Gajah, known as the Elephant Cave, an ancient Buddhist hermitage dating back to the 11th Century A.D. The fountains and pool there were unearthed as late as 1954. A huge volcanic mountain, Gunung Agung, dominates the whole northeastern end of Bali. After lying dormant for over one hundred years it suddenly erupted in 1963, killing thousands of people and wiping out entire villages. We drove for miles across its lava fields and visited the crater lake, with its boiling sulfa baths.

At the shop and workrooms of master sculptor I. Made Ada, giant carvings of the sacred Garuda bird and other exotic carved and painted forms filled several rooms. Many of his carvings are sold as special orders and shipped world-wide at a handsome price.

Unlike most of Indonesia, where Muslim is the dominate religion, Bali is Hindu. In Bali there are more temples than houses, and for special occasions these temples are a colorful sight, draped in bright fabrics and artful handicrafts. At each temple, we had to cover our shoulders and legs in accordance with Hindu custom. In Schuyler's case, since he was wearing shorts, this meant purchasing and donning a sarong! "Hawkers" clustered around the entrances of most of the temples, all too ready to sell sarongs as well as every kind of artifact.

On one dusty road we saw a procession of women with unwieldy pyramids of colorful fruit balanced on their heads, heading for a temple ceremony. At every dwelling and business establishment, in cities, towns, and even in the fields of the countryside, a daily fresh offering to the Gods was placed in front of the small shrine. Often this took the form of a tiny tray, woven from a palm leaf, containing rice, flowers, and a stick of burning incense.

The five of us boarded CORMORANT and began a partial circumnavigation of Bali. This was a rare opportunity to see places on this fabled island that most tourists never see. We anchored along the east coast, and enjoyed snorkeling and settling into a boat routine with five people in our 39 by 12-foot floating home. Rounding the northeastern corner of Bali with all sails up in a 35-knot breeze, our crew got a taste of real ocean sailing.

Along the north coast we anchored first off the village of Tulamben, in a tiny bay overlooked by a shrine with pillars and archways outlined against the sky. Snorkeling in a rocky point beneath the shrine we could see unusually large fish, and down the beach we joined groups of divers who had come to see the main attraction here....the wreck of a U.S. Liberty ship.

The ship had been damaged by Japanese torpedoes during World War II, and towed to this shore in hopes of salvaging it. It remained visible offshore until the devastating volcanic eruption of 1963, when it rolled over and now lies just below the surface, at a perfect depth for snorkeling or scuba diving. That night we dinghied ashore to explore the village and have dinner at a rustic Balinese beachside restaurant.

Sailing further west along the lightly populated north coast, we came to beautiful Lovina Beach, where several villages merge together and picturesque hotels dot the shore. We anchored inside a protecting reef off the village of Kalibukbuk, and went ashore for the night, finding bungalow-style rooms for $15 a night. From our room we could keep a watchful eye on CORMORANT.

We strolled the dusty roads in the town to explore the local restaurants and shops. After a smorgasbord dinner of delicious Indonesian food we enjoyed the delicate sound of the gamelan and graceful movements of Balinese dancers. Each dance tells a story, through the artful movements of feet, hands, and most especially the eyes.

We spent a few hours in Singaraja, the former capital of Bali. It used to be a major seaport, but now its harbor is in ruins. While Singaraja bustled with the same crowded and chaotic fervor we found in the rest of Indonesian cities, it had little of the old Dutch charm of its not-too-distant past.

Our final stop in Bali was in the northwestern corner at small, uninhabited Menjangan Island, a National Park. Here we had the best snorkeling of our entire trip so far. Hundreds of fish of all sizes and hues live along a magnificent coral cliff, which drops off from waist deep to two hundred feet in just a few boat lengths.

As we left Balinese waters heading for Java, we had the thrill of sailing beside two pilot whales for a few minutes and among great pods of cavorting dolphins.

SAILING IN THE SEVEN SEAS
(An island-hopping Indonesian tour)

Sheets of rain pelted us and lightning ripped the midnight sky as we raced across the Java Sea under a double reefed main. We had been sailing north in this squally weather for thirty-six hours, fighting against a southerly current. Such is the Java Sea when the monsoon season arrives. We longed for the calm of any anchorage, and the glitter of Singapore, three-hundred miles ahead.

*   *   *   *   *

Two weeks before we had pulled into the unglamorous industrial town of Probolingo on the northeast coast of Java, where we rafted alongside a wooden cargo vessel in the narrow, shallow town basin. We left Schuyler on board to guard CORMORANT, while we and the Pooles, jumped in "becaks" (bicycle rickshaws) and headed for town. From there we travelled by van up into the mountains for an overnight stay in a mountain lodge along the rim of Mount Bromo, an active volcano.

Our wake-up call the next day was at 3:30 a.m. We each bundled into everything warm we could find, as temperatures were in the mid-40's. After a quick cup of thick, strong coffee we mounted horses for the thirty minute walk down into the crater, across the "Sea of Sand" to the actual smoldering cauldron of Mount Bromo.

Each horse was guided by an Indonesian boy wrapped in a shawl to ward off the chill. As we rode single file down the narrow path to the crater floor below, it looked like a scene from Nepal. In the predawn light a heavy blanket of mist clung just above the sand, and beyond, at the crater's edge, a towering cloud of steam reached for the sky.

145

Once across the "Sea of Sand", our guides and horses waited below as we walked up the 276 steps to be on the edge of the cauldron just as the sun rose over the ridge. A spectacular sight!

We returned to Probolingo in the mid-morning and immediately set sail for Surabaya, the major port city of eastern Java. There the Pooles left us to return to Florida, and we began a two day out-processing ordeal with Indonesian officialdom. One fellow must have stamped his official seal fifty times on our multitude of paperwork. At Immigration, we waited an hour while the only person who could check us out completed his mid-day prayers.

There was no place for a boat of our size to take on fuel in heavily industrial Surabaya, so, using sign language, we enlisted local fishermen at a nearby small boat harbor to deliver fuel to us in their leaky jugs.

From Surabaya we headed into the Java Sea, where we ran into our first taste of the monsoon season. We were battered by increasing winds, turbulent seas, and squalls from all directions. After almost forty-eight hours of this weather, we had no choice but to alter course and seek shelter along the southern coast of Belitung Island.

Following an estuary for eleven miles, we anchored in totally calm waters among huge wooden sailing vessels loaded to the gunwales with timber. We watched in fascination as the crews poled these heavily laden boats to deep water, where they waited for the outgoing tide, then sailed away, with no motor.

In the mid-afternoon we heard voices and an outboard motor approaching CORMORANT. A boatload of uniformed officials had assembled to pay us a call. According to them, we were the first yacht ever to come to that harbor. Their impressions of America were based on what they had seen in reruns of "Miami Vice", so we spent an hour with ten of them on board talking about the more positive aspects of the United States.

From Belitung we nosed into the South China Sea for our final five days of sailing to Singapore, much of which was spent motoring on glassy seas. We had now sailed CORMORANT in five of the fabled Seven Seas (Timor, Banda, Flores, Java, and South China), missing only the Sulu and Celebes Seas which lay far to the north of our route.

We anchored one afternoon in the lee of Lait Island in a spot Ward thought would be quiet and well protected. It was, until dusk when an entire fleet of fifty fishing boats rigged with nets and lights for night fishing came right by us one at a time. We had anchored exactly in the path between their village and their fishing grounds! They realized it was an innocent mistake, and we exchanged greetings with each of the fifty boats in the twilight parade. At dawn, they all filed past again, headed home with baskets bulging with the night's catch.

Two days later we anchored in squally weather at dawn, just above the Equator. Ward and Schuyler took the dinghy ashore to fill fuel jugs for the remaining miles to Singapore. They followed a winding stream to where it intersected with the main road. Along the stream the outboard motor failed, so they found themselves rowing the final three miles upstream. There, with twenty gallons of fuel on board, they hired one of the local fishermen to tow them back downstream and out to CORMORANT.

Our last night before reaching Singapore was spent anchored just off Soreh Island in the middle of Riat Straits. It was in these islands during World War II that a daring Australian raiding party had based themselves, paddling kayaks twenty miles to attach limpet mines to Japanese shipping anchored at Singapore. They destroyed over 37,000 tons of shipping before being tracked down and killed, fighting to the last from the trees of Soreh Island.

We entered the shipping crossroads of the world, the

Straits of Singapore, at mid-day. As expected, shipping was well controlled and constant, coming and going in very distinct patterns. We crossed the shipping lanes and at one point dodged behind a freighter, sped in front of a tug towing a barge of sand, then ducked in behind another freighter coming from the opposite direction, all while we were under full sail.

We left Indonesia behind as we entered the waters of the island nation of Singapore and dropped anchor just beyond the Changi Sailing Club, which would be our home base for the next two weeks.

Ward, Peter, and Carla enjoy a game of Scrabble in Indonesia

SOUTHEAST ASIA STOP
(Even tidy Singapore has rats)

You would never find a piece of chewing gum stuck to your shoe in modern-day Singapore. Gum chewing is forbidden by law, as is smoking in public places. This tiny island-nation is "squeaky clean".

Located at the tip of the Malay Peninsula, about sixty miles north of the Equator, the island is about twenty miles across at the widest point, and fourteen miles from north to south. More than 2.5 million people live here, so it is no wonder that most of them live in high rise buildings. The population is seventy-seven percent Chinese, with the rest a mix of Malay, Indonesian, and a very small percentage of Caucasian. Gaining independence in 1965, Singapore had been a British colony since 1819 when Sir Stamford Raffles first arrived.

Efficiency is apparent everywhere, especially in the vast Mass Rapid Transit railway system and the intricate bus system. Large, clean, modern buses and sleek, fast trains (no graffiti!) can take you anywhere you want to go. As a result, very few people own cars. Since CORMORANT was anchored several miles from the downtown area, we used both systems regularly, crowding in among masses of Singaporeans for the forty-five minute ride to the city center.

In Singapore we did not have to boil our drinking water as we did in Indonesia. Modern supermarkets offered nearly everything we needed and restaurants had high quality, low priced food, especially seafood. When we tired of the local Chinese fare there was always a Burger King, Kentucky Fried Chicken, Pizza Hut or McDonalds nearby!

One has to look hard for signs of Singapore's gracious colonial days. Tucked away among towering buildings is the old Raffles Hotel, sprawling over a city block and restored to its former grandeur. Like almost all the tourists who visit the Raffles, we sipped an outrageously priced "Singapore Sling" at the famous Long Bar, where it was first concocted in 1915.

A block away, the beautiful Gothic-style St Andrews Cathedral occupies its own city block, but the remainder of the downtown seemed to be glitzy, modern buildings with more under construction. Most of the historic buildings had been leveled to make way for modern-day Singapore.

Newly developed Sentosa Island, just a two-minute ferry ride from downtown, offers attractions for tourists and Singaporeans alike. A cable car ride to Sentosa affords a bird's-eye view of the magnificent city and harbor, and once there you can ride around the island by monorail. Fort Sentosa, from where the British mistakenly had all their guns pointing toward the sea when the Japanese invaded by land in 1942, is perched on the southernmost point. Our favorite attraction on Sentosa Island was the historic wax museum, "Pioneers of Singapore", where life-sized figures depict important events such as the signing of the treaty giving Singapore back to the British in 1945.

We took a day off from working on the boat to visit the Jurong Bird Park, where more than 3,000 varieties of exotic birds from around the world are displayed in natural settings covering several acres. In a daily show pelicans, emus, flamingoes, and parrots perform tricks like circus animals.

CORMORANT was anchored, along with ten other cruising boats, close to a well-manicured public park where a short dinghy ride ashore landed us near public showers and telephones. We made good use of both. It was a ten-minute walk to the bus and a little further to neighborhood stores and restaurants, all housed in the first floor of look-alike high rise apartment buildings. In the opposite direction we would dinghy to the Changi Sailing Club, ten minutes away, and shop in still-picturesque Changi Village. Both of these long treks became tiresome, especially when lugging laundry or groceries, so we did not mind moving on after just ten days in Singapore.

Unfortunately the cleanliness of Singapore did not extend out into the water. We have never seen so many plastic bags and other garbage float by an anchorage. One night we even had an unwelcome guest on board....a small water rat that must have crawled up the anchor chain. We caught him in a trap and when Ward threw him overboard he dove into the murky, gray water. We were all too glad to leave Singapore!

Many of the other boats with us there were friends from our sailing days in Australia, and we were glad to catch up with them. In company with Shirley and Brian on MUMTAZ, from Melbourne, we hoisted anchor early one morning and motored through the bustling Singapore Harbor.

This is the busiest harbor in the world, with over five hundred ships at anchor, and others arriving and leaving constantly. Many were gigantic oil tankers arriving in a steady stream from the Middle East, loaded with crude oil for the huge refineries in Singapore. It wasn't until late in the afternoon that we motored past the last ship at anchor and headed into the Malaccan Straits.

We had heard much about the Malaccan Straits; stories of pirates and, of course, the heavy shipping. This year there was no pirating of any yachts, and the ships were all well off to our port side. Motoring through light winds we anchored along the shore each night, often awakening to the sound of fishing boats, anxious for us to leave so they could lay their nets. Further out, we picked our way around many little flags bobbing in the water, marking the nets.

One night we anchored near an island off the old city

of Malacca, where we joined up with Randall and Sharon of SARACEN from San Francisco and Dorf and Jan of KAILUA from Australia. Hailing a "bumboat" to take us to the mainland, we rode a crowded bus into the city for a day of sightseeing.

This picturesque, old place has much to offer, with its rich history of first Portuguese, then Dutch, then British occupation. An excellent museum housed in an old red-painted Dutch building, the Stadthuys, has rooms full of small dioramas accurately depicting nearly every decade of events from 1400 to the present.

Red brick Christ Church, built by the Dutch in 1763, dominates the city square. Brides and grooms, in western wedding attire, posed for pictures in this historic outdoor setting, one couple after the other. On a nearby hill stand the ruins of a fort that had been in both Portuguese and Dutch hands.

A call from Malacca to our daughter, Sally Barstow and her husband, Mark in Franklin, New York brought the joyful news of the birth of their daughter, Charlotte Anne, just thirty-six hours earlier. We stepped inside historic Christ Church to give thanks to the Lord for this gift of new life, our sixth grandchild.

KUALA LUMPUR, A SHINING CITY
(Malaysian capital is both historic and modern)

We had intended to hurry through Malaysia to allow ourselves more time in Thailand, but we found the country and people to be so delightful, we lingered for several weeks and wished for more.

Figuring there would be safety in numbers, we continued up the Straits of Malacca with SARACEN, KAILUA and MUMTAZ. Two days after leaving Malacca we passed through the narrowest portion of the Straits and pulled into Port Kelang, which is the port for Kuala Lumpur, the capital of Malaysia, an hour's bus ride away.

Before Schuyler left us at Kuala Lumpur to continue on his backpacking travels to Thailand and Australia, the three of us enjoyed two days in this magnificent city. Wide, tree-lined streets, glittering office buildings, modern shopping centers, and a charming blend of Muslim, Hindu and Western cultures make this a vibrant, cosmopolitan city.

Unlike Singapore, Kuala Lumpur (or "KL", as most people refer to it) kept many of the old buildings as it modernized, and still has a lingering old-world charm to it. The ornate Moorish-style architecture of the railroad station and City Hall, built by the British in the late 1800's, are in sharp contrast to a backdrop of glass and steel skyscrapers.

The British ruled here for over sixty years, ending with the independence of Malaya in 1957. By 1963 Malaysia came into being as the north Borneo states of Sabah and Sarawak, along with Singapore, became a Federation. Singapore became independent in 1965, and Malaysia entered into a period of internal strife as the people grappled with their future.

At the huge, modernistic National Mosque, completed

153

in 1968, Judy and Schuyler were required to put on heavy, long black robes, provided at the entrance for people wearing shorts. All female visitors were given shawls to cover their heads, and shoes had to be left outside.

Kuala Lumpur has a vast system of gardens and parks, with immaculately trimmed shrubbery and flowers bordering the avenues. We visited the Butterfly Gardens, where we walked among hundreds of varieties of butterflies, moths, and other insects, all living in the large, netted enclosure.

Stalls selling colorful fabrics and goods line the side streets by the hundreds. Malaysian women all look like they are going to a party in their long, silky two-piece outfits. The Muslim women wear a head scarf, covering all but the face.

As in most other countries we have visited which were once ruled by the British, an orderliness prevails in the systems that remain. The trains run on time, queues form for taxis and buses, and most people speak English. The tropical climate and happy mix of Malay, Chinese, Indian, and other races make this a beautiful, engaging city. One friendly Muslim woman even paid our bus fare as she showed us the way to the post office.

We said good-bye to Schuyler and returned to COR-MORANT to set sail from the Royal Selangor Yacht Club at Port Kelang for Langkawi, the northern-most island group in Malaysia. Langkawi is a Duty Free Port where we would replenish our supplies before heading on to Thailand. We sailed there through the night, regretfully by-passing the popular and historic island of Penang.

At Langkawi, we anchored just fifty yards off a green-covered, soaring volcanic islet, no other boats in view. At dawn, we dinghied ashore to an apparently unused pier and walked ten minutes down a narrow path to a fresh water lake. To our astonishment, just as we reached the isolated lake, behind us came a steady stream of tourists from Taiwan, who had been brought to the pier in small boats from their hotels. We waited twenty minutes before we could climb back up the rocky trail as over two-hundred people filed down to join us at the lake front!

We re-anchored at Kuah, the port area on the main island of Langkawi, and enjoyed this busy, rural town. It was bedecked with lights and flowers for "Deepavali", the Hindu Festival of Lights. The Langkawi area has hundreds of islands, making it a sailing paradise, similar to Vava'u in Tonga and the Virgin Islands in the Caribbean. We had time to stop at only two of the islands, and added Langkawi to the growing list of places we want to revisit.

As we left Malaysia we sailed immediately into the waters of the Kingdom of Thailand. We took three days to sail to Phuket, stopping one night at the tiny island of Rok Nok where we sought shelter from 35-knot winds and rising seas. Six Thai fishing boats joined us in a small bay, tucked in under the mountainous peak of Rok Nok. There it was absolutely calm, while 100 yards away, just past a point of land, the wind and sea howled.

On a fresh breeze, with a double reef in our mainsail, we sailed the remaining fifty miles to Phuket, an island adjoining the western-most corner of the Thailand peninsula.

THAILAND TOUR
(Bond, buses, and Bangkok)

As we sailed into Phuket, Thailand we finally caught up with sailing friends who had continued on from Darwin, Australia when we had gone back to the U.S. for two months. We joined most of them at anchor at the Ban Nit Marina, a misnomer if there ever was one. The "marina" turned out to be a thatched-roof building which served as a bar, restaurant, office, and repair shop for yachts. Run by an American yachtsman, Bob Stevens, it turned out to be just right.

Almost daily, we would dinghy ashore through a narrow pass in the fringing reef that Bob had carved out by hand. We tried to time our trips ashore for high tide; at low tide boaters had to drag or carry their dinghies fifty yards over the partially exposed coral reef. Often we hitch-hiked to nearby Phuket Town, ten miles away, to find provisions or parts for the boat, and to make phone calls. Fast-moving traffic and confusing streets made this busy town a challenge to negotiate, but we found most of the items we needed.

Thailand has its own unique alphabet. To us, all street names, shop signs, and other posted information were written in undecipherable "curly-q's". A phrase book, like the one we used in Malaysia, was useless in Thailand because many words had five meanings, depending on the level of the tone used in speaking. Fortunately, many people spoke English.

On Christmas Day an international "pot luck" feast was held at the marina, with more than sixty yachters contributing a native dish; plum pudding and Yorkshire pie from English boats, and roast turkey and pumpkin pie made by Americans were a few of the delicious fares. Since Thailand is primarily a Buddhist country, signs of

Christmas were hard to come by. We created our own in this tropical spot, even "dressing ship", by raising all our colorful signal flags from stem to stern.

An island connected to the elbow-bend of the Thai peninsula by a bridge, Phuket is fast becoming a tourist mecca, with an international airport, first-class beaches on the Andaman Sea, and glittering hotels luring people from around the world. We found the sailing on the east side of Phuket Island to be excellent and as scenic as any place we have seen.

In Phanang Bay dozens of islands jut straight up out of very shallow and calm waters. We anchored with SARACEN and KAILUA within fifty yards of these volcanic promontories. Often we found the depth in Phanang Bay too shallow for CORMORANT.

One day we engaged a fisherman to take us in his shallow draft "long-tail". These dugout-style launches have a long outboard propeller shaft which extends nearly horizontally, and send a water spray upwards as they move about the shallow waters. One of the more spectacular spots we visited was "James Bond Island", where *The Man With the Golden Gun* was filmed.

In our three dinghies the six of us paddled through the entrance of a cave at the base of a sheer cliff right by our anchorage. Stalactites, the products of hundreds of years, hung like huge animal carcasses along the edge of the island and framed the cave entrance. We worked our way through the half-mile long, twisting corridor, pitch black except for our flashlights. Dozens of bats clung to the ceiling as we glided quietly past. When one of our oars scraped the cave wall awakening them, the bats took flight in their sightless, swooshing way. Finally, we saw light at the end of the cave and emerged into an open air cathedral of greenery and water and blue sky. We were in a *hong*, the volcanic crater inside the island.

The ancient kingdom of Siam changed its name to

Thailand in 1939, becoming a constitutional monarchy, and signs of the old culture abound in this land that was never colonized by a European power. We travelled to the capital city of Bangkok for a closer look at some of them. In this vast, glittering, and crowded city, a growing problem of traffic gridlock with its noise and pollution almost obliterates the lure of the ancient temples and palaces. The splendor of those awesome sights was worth the hassle of getting there, however. Bangkok has about forty Buddhist temple-monasteries, and the saffron robes and shaved heads of monks are a common sight on the city sidewalks.

Inside the Wat Phra Kaew, a walled area containing ancient temples, we were dwarfed by the spectacular golden shape of the Reclining Buddha, measuring over forty yards. Adjacent to the temple complex is the Grand Palace, built in the late 1700's. This walled enclosure contains not only the ancient royal residences, but temples, fortifications, and a magnificent gold-encrusted chapel.

Inside the chapel is the Emerald Buddha, carved of jade and seated high upon a golden altar. Colorful, gold-trimmed buildings with sharply vaulted, fancy rooftops and ornate carvings on every facade fill the palace area. Other temples, similarly decorated, are scattered throughout the city and form a unique backdrop for the noisy traffic.

At night the sidewalks of Bangkok come alive with shoppers and vendors hawking their wares from makeshift booths lining the way. Shirts and pants, counterfeits of well-known name brands, are popular items, as well as leather goods and all sorts of craft items. Bargaining continues well into the night.

We travelled to and from Bangkok by overnight bus, stopping frequently at giant, noisy road-houses where spicy noodle and rice dishes are served at all hours of the night and day. With horn shrieking, our bus barrelled down the narrow highway, passing almost every vehicle in sight. We tried not to look.

At dawn on our return trip all passengers were deposited at an outdoor cafe in a small seaside town to wait for a connecting bus. It was fascinating to watch as the place came to life, with farmers bringing their vegetables to the nearby open market in oxcarts, and fishing boats arriving at the wharf with the night's catch. That three hundred mile trip took us nearly twenty-four hours, with changes and delays, but we got a look at some of the breathtaking mountain scenery on the Thai peninsula.

Thailand's low airfares and proximity to Vietnam and Hong Kong allowed us to squeeze in a three day visit to each of these intriguing places before setting sail across the Indian Ocean.

A RETURN VISIT TO VIETNAM
(Ward served here in 1962 and again in 1968)

As we landed at Tan Son Nhat Airport (new spelling brought in by North Vietnam), we both felt like we were stepping into the unknown; would Vietnam be hostile to Americans or would we be welcome?

In the same building where Ward had first arrived thirty-two years before, we now looked into the eyes of very solemn, curt, meticulous, young Immigration officials, who hadn't even been born in 1962. This introduction to Vietnam was formal and proper, and left us, the only Americans on our plane, feeling accepted but not really welcome.

Soon we were settled into a modest hotel, right in the heart of downtown Saigon (officially called Ho Chi Minh City in honor of the wartime President of North Vietnam). It was here that American Advisors lived during their first few days after arrival in the early 1960's. Surprisingly, Saigon's appearance had changed very little, which correctly implied that there hadn't been much post-war growth.

The charm that had made Saigon the "Paris of the Orient" was gone, and while the people seemed just as nice and friendly as in the past, there was now an aloofness in their attitude. Certainly not hostile, the population had, however, been "re-educated" by the North Vietnamese and their cautious though curious approach to us reflected that.

The traditional Vietnamese dress, the flowing "ao dai" with its silky tunic over long pants, has all but disappeared, now seen mostly on bank and hotel clerks as a sort of costume. Women in black pants, short tunics and conical hats still scurry through the streets carrying heavily laden buckets suspended from both ends of

160

a pole over their shoulder. Most people, however were in western dress, and anything American was "in"; from music to jeans to tee-shirts.

The same wide, tree-lined boulevards and grand hotels which had served as Bachelor Officers' Quarters during the war were there. The one major improvement we did notice was the upgrading of those hotels, some even to four-star ratings. An elegant five-star floating hotel, bought from Australia, was now the center of attraction on the riverfront, and most tourists (mainly Europeans) seemed to stay there.

We were pedalled in one-seater *cyclos* (three-wheeled bicycle rickshaws) throughout Saigon and Cholon, the Chinese section of the city. This turned out to be an excellent way to see the sights and keep up with the traffic, which was almost entirely bicycle, motor bike, and pedestrian.

At the Vietnamese War Museum, all the "crimes" of the American forces were documented. One entire room was devoted to the Agent Orange results. The American Embassy, where such graphic photographs of the last hours for the U.S. in Vietnam were taken, is now the office for a petroleum company.

We were surprised that there were no restrictions placed on our travels, and one day we hired a car with an English-speaking driver to take us out of Saigon. Driving north along Highway 13, we saw the places Ward had been as an Advisor in the early days of the war.

We stopped at the little village of Bau Bang, where Ward had first been dropped off by helicopter to join his Vietnamese battalion in the field. Now thatched-roofed shops and homes line the roadside. At a small cafe where we stopped for a mid-morning break, we found teen-aged boys singing Karaoke-style, using a microphone and video tape with English words subtitled. Why they weren't in school or at work remains a puzzling question.

The Lai Khe airstrip, where helicopters used to shuttle

South Vietnamese troops in and out, and where Judy's letters arrived twice-weekly on small Army airplanes, was now completely overgrown, unrecognizable as an airfield. The surrounding rubber plantation was being cut down for use as lumber. Gone too was the nearby "strategic hamlet" which Ward had helped defend; the nearby French dairy and plantation houses had vanished. The former headquarters of the U.S. 1st Infantry Division, which had been at Lai Khe, was in disrepair but still in use by a Vietnamese military organization.

We stopped for lunch of mei soup (noodles and broth) in the village of Ben Cat, scene of dozens of battles during the war. It was a treat to spend an hour with smiling, happy Vietnamese children at a family-run roadside cafe. The traffic was primarily ox driven carts, and an occasional bus, loaded down with everything from bicycles to chickens, and overflowing with people. Now the only military presence in Ben Cat is a Viet Cong War Memorial Cemetery.

Back in Saigon we went to the Municipal Theater to watch a three-hour variety show. The entrance fee was only a dollar. We had an elegant meal at popular Maxim's restaurant, complete with elaborate floor show, all at a very reasonable rate. One evening we took a dinner cruise down the Saigon River on one of four fancy river boats, for a view of the city by night.

On a balmy Sunday evening we strolled down Lei Loi street for an ice cream and found hordes of motor bikes, bicycles and pedestrians filling the streets. Hundreds of them repeatedly circled the six or eight blocks of the center of town at a gridlock pace. Happy and smiling, often with entire families on one motorbike, it seemed that all of Saigon was there for this three-hour outing which has become a weekend ritual.

During a day trip down the Saigon River we were impressed with the number of ships at moorings in mid-channel and the dozens of smaller craft. Most of the ocean-going vessels were from Eastern Block countries and China. Our little boat took us up side estuaries into the heart of Cholon, where makeshift houses crowded the riverside.

Here the river was black with oil and filthy, yet people were wading neck deep, hunting for mussels with their toes. Twice our boat skipper had to lower himself into the murky waters to clear debris from the fouled propeller.

In spite of the poor, impoverished conditions that exist throughout Vietnam, the people appear industrious. Their constant enigmatic smiles seemed to say; "Give us time, and we'll put this country back." English has replaced Russian and French language instruction in the school system, a clear indication of the direction Vietnam intends to take.

A U.S. Senate delegation was in Vietnam at the same time we were, deciding what to recommend to the U.S. President about the trade embargo. We were delighted when several weeks later the embargo was lifted. U.S. commerce will now flow in and provide a much needed boost to the Vietnamese economy. Now perhaps we can truly put the war behind us, as well we should.

HONG KONG: JEWEL OF THE ORIENT
(Ready for changes in July, 1997)

When our Cathay Pacific jet touched down at nine in the evening at the busy Kai Tak airport in Hong Kong, we didn't know where we would be staying for our three days in this exciting place. After clearing through Customs and Immigration, we made a quick phone call to the Mariners' Club, and were assured they would hold a room for us. It turned out to be a perfect place for two sailors carrying their packs, ready for the fast pace of this fascinating metropolis.

Living aboard CORMORANT qualified us to take advantage of the Mariners' Club, located in downtown Kowloon on Middle Road, near the glitzy Holiday Inn and the stately Peninsula Hotel. It offers clean, comfortable rooms and a homey atmosphere for seamen as well as nicely appointed "married quarters", a dining room, lounge rooms, and a chapel, all at a reasonable rate.

A British colony since the mid-1800's, Hong Kong will become part of the Peoples' Republic of China on the 1st of July, 1997 when England's ninety-nine year lease runs out. There are about six hundred square miles of land in Hong Kong and almost six million people. Most of them are squeezed into the sprawling city of Kowloon, and the island of Hong Kong. The New Territories, which includes the Outer Islands, make up the rest of Hong Kong.

On the Star Ferry one morning we crowded along with the rush of office workers on their way from Kowloon across the narrow, busy harbor to Hong Kong Island, the business center of Hong Kong. Exotically shaped glass and steel skyscrapers lined the approaching shoreline and spread up the surrounding hills.

Buses, cars, and the high-speed subway travel

through newly constructed tunnels under the harbor, helping to move over a million people daily. All of this hustle and bustle being done in relative comfort recognizes the successful blending of Chinese temperament and British efficiency. It seemed as if every person had a telephone growing out of his or her ear as the cellular age allowed the business of Hong Kong to be transacted non-stop, in buses, ferries, or on the sidewalks.

A double-decker bus took us over hills to a more rural area on the far side of Hong Kong Island. Along the winding road at the edge of the cliff we passed the beautiful resort area and beach of Repulse Bay, and Aberdeen, where a "floating village" of sampans used to house thousands of people. Further out on a spit of land is the town of Stanley, and at the end of the line is a small British Army post, with soldiers guarding the gates, smartly dressed in Black Watch plaid kilts.

Surely the most popular attraction on the island of Hong Kong is Victoria Peak, from where the whole harbor and all of Kowloon can be viewed over the tops of the skyscrapers. A nearly vertical tram took us up the side of the mountain to the chilly, windy summit, where the sights were visible even on a foggy day.

While on Hong Kong island we sought out the Chinese Consulate to get a visa for a one day trip to mainland China. Most people do this by taking an expensive guided tour, but we prefer to make our own way. We put "journalist" on the printed form as our occupation, since we write monthly for the Free Lance-Star, rather than "retired", which we usually put, thinking it would expedite the processing time. We were then told that while tourists could travel alone, because we were "journalists" we would have to join a guided tour. No amount of logic could convince the Chinese man in charge that we were really just tourists. We left the Consulate feeling more keenly aware of the cold obstinacy and xenophobia that prevails within the government of China.

165

As it turned out, roaming about the "shoppers' paradise" of Kowloon filled our two remaining days in Hong Kong, and we were just as glad not to have made the day-long, controlled tour to China.

One night we took the subway to the renown Temple Street Market, where each evening the street fills with vendors' stalls selling everything from clothes to electronic gear, all at rock-bottom prices. We ate fried rice at one of the cluttered sidewalk restaurants and both got sick. We bought some medicine whose label we could not read, and spent the next twenty-four hours in our room recovering. The Chinese pharmacist had assured us that the small yellow pills would quickly cure the problem, and they did.

One evening we strolled into the grand, old Peninsula Hotel, now deprived of its waterfront view by a modernistic, round museum building and dwarfed by newer high-rise hotels. People sipped coffee and ate dessert at tables in the elegant lobby as a string quartet serenaded them from the mezzanine above, a touch of the elegance of old Hong Kong. Nearby in the streets of Kowloon a colorful jungle of neon lights glared above the noisy traffic and busy sidewalks. Across the channel the towers of Hong Kong bristled with lights reflecting off the water.

On Nathan Road, the main thoroughfare of Kowloon, a handsome mosque, a Chinese temple, and a quaint Anglican church occupy the same block, all in perfect harmony. We attended an early morning service at St. Andrews Church and learned that nine percent of the population is Christian, while the huge majority in Hong Kong practice a mix of the Chinese religions of Taoism, Buddhism, and Confucianism.

We were thankful for the opportunity to visit Hong Kong before this tiny enclave of capitalism is turned over to China. The eyes of the world will be watching to see what will change here after July 1997. We think that Hong Kong will actually lead the rest of China towards capitalism and greater human rights.

Schuyler Sweet and Judy weather a storm in the Java Sea

Touring Saigon by cyclo

With Charlie & Pat Poole on Bali

Headed for a temple ceremony in Bali

168

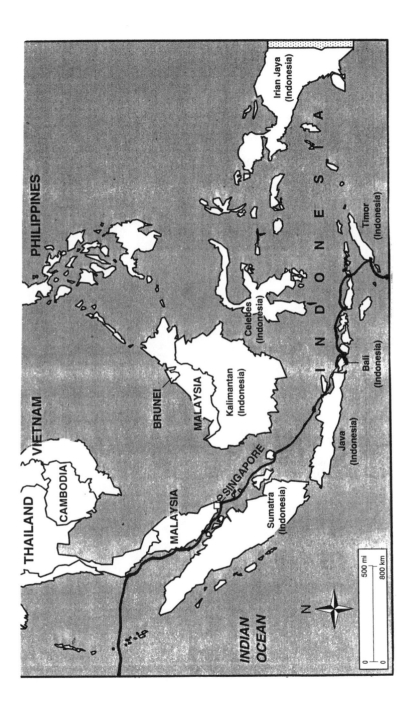

THAILAND TO CYPRUS

"Day after day, day after day,
We stuck, not breath nor motion;
As idle as a painted ship
Upon a painted ocean."

From Part II of:"The Rime of the Ancient Mariner"
by Samuel Taylor Coleridge

THE BAY OF BENGAL AND SRI LANKA
(Calm seas, tea and elephants)

Ahead of us lay the ink-blue unknown of the Indian Ocean. At this latitude (eight degrees north), the 3,000 mile passage between Thailand and Aden (Yemen) would include crossing the Bay of Bengal and the Arabian Sea. We decided to break up the trip with an extended stop at Sri Lanka, the tear-drop shaped island nation off the southeastern tip of India.

Every year the waters of the Bay of Bengal spawn devastating cyclones that reap havoc in Bangladesh. In February, the month we picked to cross, no cyclones have ever been reported. The seas were often so calm there wasn't a ripple to disturb the gently undulating blue.

When the breeze freshened, we could sail "wing and wing" for hours at a time. "John Miller", our faithful wind vane did all the work to keep us on course. In our quiet nine day crossing we had only a brief squall, saw one ship, no dolphins and very little debris. One day our only excitement was a small plastic chair that floated by!

A strange phenomenon overcomes ocean sailors: after a week at sea you can't wait to get to shore; after a week ashore, you long for the freedom of the sea. At twilight of our eighth day at sea, Sri Lanka loomed twenty miles off our bow. We were anxious to be anchored at Galle Harbor.

That night, ships and small boats converged on the southern tip of Sri Lanka like bees to honey. We felt as if we were in a traffic jam. More than twenty ships were on our radar screen as we rounded Dondra Head, and headed up the west coast to Galle. Smaller fishing boats with their dim lights added to the hazard. We gave the shore an even wider berth than planned as we waited for dawn before entering the harbor.

Sri Lanka, formerly known as Ceylon, was controlled by foreign rule for the last four centuries. Its strategic location along the world's sea lanes made it a key possession for first the Portuguese, then the Dutch, and then the British. The island regained its independence in 1948, and in 1972 retrieved from 2,500 years of history the ancient name of Sri Lanka, which means Splendid Land. The inhabitants of Sri Lanka embraced Buddhism over 2,300 years ago and it remains the predominant religion of the island.

On a three-day trip inland with Jack and Heather from WIRRAWAY and Phil and Fay from GOLDEN APPLE, we travelled by van into the highlands to the small city of Kandy. Here the Temple of the Tooth Relic attracts believers and tourists in droves. It is said that a portion of one of Buddha's teeth is enshrined in the temple. We witnessed the elaborate Changing of the Guard in the temple and saw the ornate rooms surrounding the Tooth Sanctuary. At a Sri Lankan dance presentation, entertainers dressed in ancient costumes portrayed the beliefs and customs of the people.

More than forty elephants live at the Elephant Orphanage, and we followed them to the river for their daily bath. They lie down in waist deep water, often with only the tip of their trunk waving in the air like a strange serpent, while their bulk is underwater.

Elephants are still used to move heavy items and more than once we stopped our van to watch them lifting logs. Water buffaloes at work in the rice paddies, wild monkeys, cascading waterfalls, and the spectacular mountain scenery of central Sri Lanka kept us entertained.

A large portion of the world's tea is produced in the hills of Sri Lanka. At the famous Ceylon Tea Plantation, where acres of green leafy bushes paraded across the upper slopes in unending rows, clusters of tea leaf pick-ers bent to their never-ending task. We learned that only the top three leaves and a bud are picked, and new ones sprout every two weeks. The leaves are then sorted, boiled, ground, and sorted again, with the poorest quality destined for the familiar individual tea bags.

Back in Galle we spent several hours catching up with other cruisers over beers on the veranda of Don Windsor's home, close by the harbor. Don, who was a native of Sri Lanka, Anglicized his name while studying in Hong Kong. He has become a legend within the cruising world, having befriended yachtsmen for over twenty years until his death in 1991. Now his sons, Vinnie and Santosh, maintain the business, which provides not only hospitality but also provisions, overseas telephone service, and a fax machine. They also do most of the paperwork needed to clear a yacht in and out of the country, all for a reasonable fee.

The old city of Galle hides behind the massive walls of the fortress guarding the harbor. Established by the Portuguese and improved on by the Dutch and British, the fortress now contains offices, banks, museums, post offices, and Catholic, Anglican and Dutch Reform churches. At the New Oriental Hotel, with its high ceilings, slowly whirling fans, and arched windows open to the balmy air, we enjoyed lemonade on the veranda and an elegant meal for just a few dollars.

In the "modern" section of Galle, we found everything from oil filters to plastic water jugs, and a bustling outdoor marketplace. Women in bright flowing "saris" added a splash of color everywhere we looked.

We used public buses for the five minute ride from the harbor into town. It meant standing up packed like sardines, but for just four cents a ride we figured we could endure. At the modern post office we experienced the Sri Lankan habit of not waiting in line for service; they cluster at the counter like cattle at a gate.

During our stay at anchor in Galle, we discovered

that salt water was collecting in the fuel tanks each time we tried to run the engine. Phil and Jack came over to try to identify the cause of the leak, to no avail. Finally we discovered that a salt-water cooling system in the fuel line had corroded, allowing the mix of fluids.

Several days were required to blow all the fuel lines, clean and pressure test the fuel injectors, and separate the salt water from the fuel in the tanks. We siphoned fuel into pans, then drained good fuel from the top and discarded the water and contaminated fuel that lay at the bottom. Since we had just filled our fuel tanks, the process was a long and messy one, but fortunately we found that no damage had been done to the engine. With the removal of the fuel cooling system and a new fuel hose in place, we sailed off into the Arabian Sea.

ACROSS THE ARABIAN SEA
(A stop at the pristine Maldives)

Between Sri Lanka and Aden lies the Arabian Sea. This would be our second longest passage so far, and our longest one alone.

Soon after leaving Galle Harbor we noticed three small rips in our genoa jib, apparently caused as the giant sail brushed past the inner forestay when we tacked. This provided us with an excuse (sail repair) to stop in the Republic of Maldives, five-hundred miles away. That unexpected stop proved to be one of our most interesting.

The thousand-plus islands of the Republic of Maldives, of which only two hundred are inhabited, are strung out in the Indian Ocean for over five hundred miles, north to south. Except for brief Portuguese occupation in the 16th century, this peaceful Muslim country has remained independent. Of Indian extraction, Maldivians have dark skin, shiny black hair, and a gentle and honest nature.

We sailed into a small bay at the northernmost island, Turakunu, a two-square-mile speck set in azure waters. Not knowing what to expect, we motored towards the shore. We could see a tidy white building set back in the trees, and on the beach a woman in a long flowing dress seemed to be frantically waving us away. We decided to keep going and anchored at a smaller, deserted island nearby.

Soon a fishing boat powered our way, and four friendly youths jumped on board to welcome us in English and ask us to move CORMORANT back to the first anchorage. As it turned out, the woman on the beach had been waving us in, not shooing us away. This was to be the start of a memorable three days, since we were the first sailboat to visit that year.

The formalities of checking in with the authorities were accomplished easily when another native boat soon came out, full of island officials and more curious youths. Though technically we should have checked in at the capital of Male, two hundred miles to the south, we were told that we could stay as long as we wished, and they invited us ashore.

Our new young friends, Mohamud, Ibrahim, and Shaucut paid us a visit later that day dressed in crisp, clean shirts and pants, and would not take even so much as a glass of water. It was Ramadan, the solemn annual Muslim observance during which they fasted until sundown each day for a month. This was a welcome change from officials in Sri Lanka, who had asked us outright for coke, beer, cigarettes, and even tee-shirts.

We were taken ashore in a large fishing boat the following day along with Sonia and Dixon, American friends on RIVA who arrived a day behind us. They are both doctors and generously offered to conduct a clinic for the island people. Mohamud and Ibrahim interpreted for them as they treated the ailments of more than thirty people.

Most of the boys and men of the village seemed to be on shore waiting to greet the four of us. We were given cool, fresh coconuts to drink and ushered to a long row of seats lashed together under the trees. Sonia and Judy had covered their arms and legs in deference to Muslim custom for women. We noticed the absence of women and girls, and learned that they spend most of the time in their homes doing chores and caring for the children.

Followed by a growing stream of small boys, we roamed immaculate, broad sand and coral walkways bordered by bending palm trees. Women and girls dressed in colorful, long silky dresses peeked at us from the doorways of immaculate homes made with white coral blocks and mortar.

When our escort, Shaucut and his friend left us briefly to pray in one of the three mosques at the appointed hour, we wandered to a small hut and found two beautiful, long-haired women cooking bread rounds over small underground "burners". They giggled and happily allowed us to take their picture.

Other groups of women and girls vanished into the doorways when they saw our cameras, but a few agreed to pose for us, like the friendly Family Health Nurse. She is the one we thought had been waving us away when we first sailed in.

There are no vehicles or animals on the island, except for a few chickens. The neatness and cleanliness amazed us, as well as the healthy appearance and tidy dress of these more than six hundred handsome people. We saw a modern elementary school building, and learned that the older children are taken to another island for further education. Some, like Mohamud and Ibrahim, attend the university in Male.

The islanders were proud of the newest *dhonis*, the typical Maldivian fishing boat, that had just been completed and launched. This magnificent craft, all hand-constructed, cost the equivalent of $2,000, they proudly told us. A curved, slender upward extension of the bow makes these boats uniquely Maldivian.

We remained at Turakunu an extra day for an evening fish-fry in our honor, given by several of the youths. We watched in the starlight as they caught, cleaned, and cooked several large fish, insisting that each of us haul in a fish, once they had it hooked. Seated in the sand around a large plastic sheet, we ate with our hands from palm leaves. Our hosts would not eat until we had our fill, and afterwards they performed an island dance for us, singing and beating on native drums. As a finale they presented both American couples with a delicate miniature "dhonis", skillfully carved by Mohamud's fourteen-year old brother, Ali.

Our sail repaired, we set out once again for Aden. For the first few days there were always ships on the horizon, heading through the Eight Degree Channel to and from the major port of Bombay on the western coast of India. Days were clear and the wind was gentle and constant from the east, pushing us along.

Dolphins often dove alongside of us, looking like shiny rockets in the phosphorescent night waters. Sometimes when the seas were like glass we motored, always mindful of the need to conserve fuel on such a long trip. On one such day we arranged a mid-ocean rendezvous with RIVA to exchange books, boat parts and freshly caught fish.

In the vast night sky both the Southern Cross and the North Star were visible, reminding us that we were gradually moving north from the Southern Hemisphere, where we had been for so long. We were also able to re-establish radio contact with Fred Chapman in Fredericksburg and others in the Afloat Net, which helped boost our morale with radio/telephone calls to family and friends.

Passing within twelve miles of the Horn of Africa, we entered the Gulf of Aden and shuddered at the uninviting sight of the barren, jagged sand hills of Somalia. The last American troops were leaving Somalia the day we sailed past.

One night approaching the coast of Yemen, we were caught in a blow with the jib poled out. In a rollicking sea, Ward went on deck to secure the pole at 2:00 a.m. Calm prevailed the rest of the way and we reached the ancient port of Aden twenty-five days after leaving Sri Lanka.

ADEN—GATEWAY TO THE MIDDLE EAST
(Our introduction to the Arabian peninsula)

We couldn't believe the appearance of Aden as we approached from the east. With crumbling buildings, stark rock cliffs, and a yellow-brown, sandy cast to everything, this once picturesque colony of the British Empire appeared ravaged by decades of war.

Aden is now a part of Yemen, a Socialist Arab country which supported Iraq during the 1991 Gulf War. It was therefore with some uncertainty that we sailed into Aden harbor with our American flag flying smartly in the 25-knot breeze. Years ago Aden was a major port of call for passenger ships; now it is a fueling stop for cargo ships, and the waters of the harbor shine with an oily scum.

This area has had a chaotic history, and only in the last few years has known peace. The Turks occupied Aden from 1781 to 1828. For the next 139 years, it was occupied and ruled by the British. Fighting between local and British forces broke out in 1964, ending when the British withdrew from Aden in 1967.

They were replaced by the Russians in 1972, and during that occupation no real improvements were made. A costly and destructive civil war engulfed the region from 1986 until 1989, resulting in the creation of one country, Yemen, out of South Yemen and North Yemen, and the withdrawal of the 60,000 Russians in 1990.

Once we got through the Customs and Immigration check-in we followed the advice of cruisers who had gone before us and found Omar, the taxi driver. He quickly showed us that he could be trusted and his advice relied upon completely. For the equivalent of $8.00 a day, Omar drove us around explaining the colorful history of Aden as he pointed out British landmarks and Turkish ruins.

He interpreted for us at the marketplace, took us to a local restaurant for lunch, and helped us secure visas at the Egyptian Consulate.

At one point we asked Omar to get some film developed for us and later that evening he tracked us down at a restaurant to deliver the prints. Once when we ran out of local money, Omar provided what we needed until we could pay him back.

The people on the streets of Aden were surprisingly friendly and helpful. One elderly man was proud to have been to America and insisted on giving us a gift of a bag of flour he had just purchased for himself.

In Aden, the official rate of exchange at the bank is twelve Riyals to one U.S. dollar. Everyone uses "money changers" to exchange money at the vastly more favorable rate of sixty to one. Normally when we arrive in a foreign country we get a cash advance from a bank using a credit card. That process has worked well for us worldwide—until Aden.

Since Yemen doesn't deal with any of the major credit card companies, we seemed stuck without enough cash to provision adequately. Thanks to other cruisers we found the "Toshiba Store" along the waterfront, so named because of a Toshiba advertisement in English over the door. They sold not only Toshiba products, but also frozen hot dogs and old jewelry, and sent faxes, changed money, and even cashed our personal check drawn on a U.S. bank.

With Omar as guide, twelve of us rented a van with driver to get out of Aden and see the countryside. Technically we were restricted to the harbor area, but Omar worked his magic and off we went for an eight-hour round trip to the city of Taizz, in what used to be North Yemen. At four checkpoints near the old border we were stopped by the military and the police. Each time Omar told us to keep our cameras hidden and let him do the talking. We breezed around the barricades with friendly waves from North and South Yemeni soldiers.

The barren landscape of the Arabian peninsula was breathtaking in its severity. We saw miles and miles of nothing but rock, sand, and low lying scrub brush in dry stream beds. Every twenty miles or so there would be a cluster of mud huts and nearby a herd of scraggly goats or sheep tended by children. Camels were the mode of transport for many of the men, and women in colorful veils would often appear riding donkeys. We stopped for a break in one of these larger clusters, and found that piping hot flat bread rounds with a delicious bean dip and tea served in the middle of the desert was a magnificent breakfast.

Taizz was a metropolis compared to the surrounding countryside. Cars and trucks competed equally with camels and donkeys in the heart of this mountain city. We parked the van and, loosely guided by Omar, plunged into the central market and bazaar area.

Muslim women, faces completely shielded by black veils, would be shopping for tomatoes right beside us. However, when we asked to take their picture, they objected vehemently. Yemini men, with their ceremonial curved dagger tucked in their waist sash, seemed to be the predominant shoppers.

Throughout the day and evening it was a common sight to see men with cheeks bulging, chewing a wad of green *qat* leaves. We were told that this mildly narcotic leaf provides a mellowing effect which seems to settle and soothe those who chew it. It was not unusual to smile at a vendor in the market place and have him smile back with green mush embedded in his teeth.

Back in Aden, we finished provisioning for our sail up the Red Sea. We also toured the "Queen of Sheba Baths", an ancient water cachement system built in the hills in Biblical times. It had been buried under sand and silt until its discovery by a British officer in the late 1800s.

One evening about thirty of us from ten boats met for dinner at a Chinese restaurant. The event was organized by a local British banker, Nick Hawkins and our cruising friend Pat Henry, from Southern Cross.* It was also a farewell dinner, for soon we would all sail at various times, some not linking up again until Cyprus, three months away.

Seeing parts of Yemen and being at anchor in Aden for a week caused us to reflect:

—The British Empire, which literally circled the globe, left its mark in many ways, most importantly in the widespread use of the English language. We have been following the sea lanes of the world now for almost three years and the positive British influence is apparent in the British Virgin Islands, Fiji, Australia, Singapore, Hong Kong, Malaysia, Sri Lanka and Aden.

—The Muslim world as we have seen it in Indonesia, Malaysia and the Maldives can be gentle, loving and kind with reasonable application of such things as veiling for adult women. In Yemen, however, we experienced for the first time a country bent on following Socialist doctrine and the hard-line application of Muslim protocol.

*   *   *   *   *

As we said a fond farewell to Omar and headed out of the oil-filthy harbor of Aden towards the Red Sea, it was obvious that we had entered another world— The Middle East. Here three of the world's great religions have their roots, oil riches and harsh poverty exist side by side, three continents converge, and it is in the Middle East that mistrust and lack of understanding between the West and the East are most acute.

*In 1997 Pat would become the first American woman to sail around the world singlehandedly.

A month after leaving Aden we learned that fighting had erupted between the military of North and of South Yemen, and North Yemen aircraft (Russian-built MIG 17's) were bombing the very places we had been while in Aden. We received a note from Omar telling us that the mail we had asked him to forward was destroyed when the Post Office burned following an air attack.

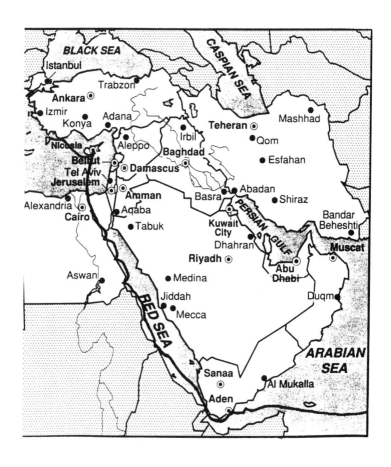

THE DAUNTING RED SEA
(Smooth sailing along Sudan; rougher in Egypt)

We approached the southern end of the Red Sea with respect and apprehension. From all we had heard and read, this 1,200-mile long, 70-mile wide sea would demand our undivided attention. Uncharted reefs, gale-force head winds, short, steep seas, howling sand storms, constant ship traffic, and unfriendly fishermen were what we anticipated.

We left Aden harbor with a filthy water line from the oil scum there. We stopped twenty miles away at a small island, known in the cruising community as "Washdown Island", where we did just that. We intended to anchor the next night overlooking the Straits of Bab El Mandeb, the southern entrance to the Red Sea.

As we prepared to drop anchor at the southwestern tip of North Yemen, we noticed bright floodlights turned our way and menacing gestures and voices from what appeared to be a military encampment there. Rather than confront this situation, we decided to sail on through the night and into the Red Sea.

Late the next day we dropped anchor at the northern tip of Zuqar Island, twenty miles off the coast of North Yemen. Inside a small lagoon we waited for two days until our Australian friends, Jack and Heather on WIRRAWAY arrived. For added security we wanted to sail up the Red Sea in company with at least one other boat.

At dawn we were approached by a Yemenese fishing boat with twelve men on board. We decided to be casual and polite, though Ward positioned our only weapon, a flare pistol, in easy reach. It turned out that they had a mechanical problem and needed to borrow a hand drill. An hour later, they had fixed their problem and returned our drill along with fresh fish and a huge, live lobster as a gift.

Mild southerly winds helped us decide to push on soon after WIRRAWAY joined us, and we sailed together for two days and nights. We stayed well offshore of Ethiopia and the newly independent country of Eritrea, until reaching our landfall...the southern end of Sudan.

At one point in the middle of the Red Sea three separate pods of dolphin joyfully raced alongside us for miles. One large dolphin rolled over on his side to get a clear look at Ward standing on the bow, then leaped out of the water landing in a belly flop, splashing Ward. As if to prove it wasn't an accident, the dolphin repeated the same moves once more before swimming away.

At delightful, uninhabited anchorages along the Sudanese coast we combed the beaches finding beautiful shells, snorkeled in warm, clear waters, and had beach bonfires and communal dinners with WIRRAWAY and yachts RACONTEUR III and RIVA who had re-joined us. It was strange to see only a few fishermen from this impoverished country where the sea abounds with fish. The bulk of the population lives along the Nile River two hundred miles inland.

While walking around Long Island, one of our many anchorages, we met six Sudanese fishermen boiling their catch of lobster in crude metal containers. We negotiated a fair price ($15) for four large ones and enjoyed a lobster roast on the beach that night with our friends.

We officially entered Sudan at the old slave trading town of Suakin. Motoring past the huge new wharf complex, we anchored just fifty feet off the shore of "old" Suakin, which dates back to 1000 B.C. It now lies in ruins and rubble from years of wars, neglect and disuse. It was from Suakin that the last slaves were sold to Saudi Arabia as late as 1948, when slave trading finally ended in Sudan.

The "new" Suakin was a ramshackle village with several two- story buildings nestled in among shacks. The dirt streets were filled with camels, goats, and donkeys.

Sudan controls visitors carefully, and we were allowed only a three-hour shore pass to buy provisions. We bought bread directly from the baker as he pulled it from an earthen stove, and stocked up on fruits and vegetables in the scruffy marketplace.

On our last visit ashore we were invited into one of the shacks by the eighty year old father of two young boys who had befriended us. We sipped strong coffee which he prepared on a pile of charcoal in the middle of the dirt floor of this one room shack, which was built into the rubble of the old town.

ASTRON, with New Zealanders Brian and Louise Pearce and fourteen year old, Hedley, joined us at Suakin, bringing a very welcome pack of mail that had missed us in Aden. Our little flotilla of five boats pushed on up the Red Sea, stopping each night at well protected coves along the coast.

At Rumi, an offshore reef where Jacques Cousteau once lived in an underwater home while studying sharks, we snorkeled in the still waters of this circular reef and had marvelous looks at Red Sea coral and fish. Further up the Sudanese coast we anchored for two days at the Taila Islands, sand spits at best, with incredibly clear waters and enormous shells.

Leaving Sudan and entering Egyptian waters during an overnight sail, now in company with seven boats, we enjoyed gentle southerly winds. At 1:00 a.m. conditions changed abruptly when a cigarette-shaped cloud appeared, stretching across the moonlit sky. It heralded a major shift of wind direction and strength and by 2:00 a.m. we were in typical Red Sea weather...35-knot winds on the nose, in hull-thumping short, steep seas.

Certain that this was the start of a lengthy pattern of bad weather, five of us sought the nearest shelter, a massive reef complex in Foul Bay, twenty-miles away. ASTRON and WIRRAWAY were far enough ahead that they decided to continue on in what turned out to be another dreadful twelve hours of pounding into sea and wind for them.

We arrived at the reef at dawn, and waited for better light to negotiate the entrance. Once we were behind the reef the seas flattened out, and we carefully picked our way through a veritable mine field of coral heads to a tiny sand spit. There we waited for four days while strong winds howled through the rigging.

Finally the winds eased, and we all quickly continued north. Knowing we had only about thirty-six hours before strong northerly winds would return, RACONTEUR III and CORMORANT kept going, hoping to reach Safaga, Egypt by dark. We had a glorious sail, and just as the town of Safaga came into view the wind picked up. Within minutes we had triple-reefed our main sail and were tacking to dodge entrance reefs as we bucked into twenty-foot swells fed by the 35-knot winds. The last four miles into Safaga took two hours, but we made it just at dusk. We enjoyed being tied to the Customs wharf, sheltered from the weather for the night, eager to experience Egypt in the coming weeks.

EGYPT: FROM THE RED SEA TO THE NILE VALLEY
(Time out to visit temples and tombs)

When we reached Safaga it was time to take a break from the rigors of the Red Sea. We decided to travel inland to the city of Luxor on the Nile River, and visit the Valley of the Kings (Pharaohs) and the magnificent ancient temples there.

Early one morning eleven of us from five different boats, RIVA, WIRRAWAY, RACONTEUR III, ASTRON, and CORMORANT, piled into a bus full of Egyptian travellers for the five-hour journey to Luxor. We crossed coastal mountains, a vast, sandy desert, and finally the green, fertile valley of the Nile.

We could soon see the many irrigation ditches distributing the Nile's water. Since the Aswan Dam was built to control flooding, farmers can now grow three crops each year. We learned that over ninety percent of Egypt's population lives in the Nile Valley, which is only three percent of Egypt's land.

Modern day Luxor, located on the east bank of the Nile, hums with noise and activity. Muslin women draped in black mix with others dressed in western attire. A mournful chanting booms over loud speakers five times a day, calling Muslims to worship. A constant jingle of bells sounds from shiny horse carriages that ply the narrow streets, their white-robed drivers looking hopefully for riders. "Hawkers" along the streets tout their wares to the few tourists in town and dozens of river boats of all sizes lie empty, tied in rows along the Nile's edge.

A terrorist scare kept the usual number of tourists away this year, but we never felt threatened and in fact were greeted in a friendly way everywhere we went. Because of the slack business, we were able to bargain for a good rate for all we did and bought. Bargaining is expected so the initial prices are often unrealistically high.

The Valley of the Kings, located on the west bank of the Nile, is where the kings of the "Middle Kingdom" and the "New Kingdom", from about 2500 B.C. until 1200 B.C., were buried. Elaborate underground tombs, cleverly hidden and dug deep into the hillsides, contained not only the mummies of the kings but dazzling arrays of possessions to accompany them into the afterlife. This was of great importance to the ancient Egyptians.

Colorful drawings, intricate carvings, and hieroglyphics covered the walls lining the long corridors. The most well known tomb is that of King Tutankhamen, discovered in 1922 by British archeologist Howard Carter. Grave robbers through the centuries have stripped most of the tombs of valuable objects. "King Tut's" tomb was discovered intact, however, and in the Egyptian Museum in Cairo we would see its remarkable contents.

We went deep into the earth down steep steps to visit the tombs of Ramses I, Ramses IV, and Horemhab, one of Tutankhamen's generals, who is believed to have killed the eighteen year old king. At the Tombs of the Nobles, less grand than the kings', we saw down-to-earth depictions of daily life in the days of the Pharaohs etched on the walls of the tombs.

Back out into the hot sun we were taken by our guide to Queen Hatshepsut's Temple, a few miles away near the Valley of the Queens. Constructed in the 16th Century B.C., this magnificent building has been studied down through the ages by architects for its simplicity and perfect balance, as well as its unique setting below sheer cliffs.

The seventy-foot high Colossi of Memnon, two gigantic statues, are all that is left of a temple built in the 14th Century B.C. by Amenhotep III, Tutankhamen's grandfather. They stand side by side on a flat plain not far from the Nile. Flooding throughout the centuries completely destroyed the temple.

Back in Luxor we rode in a horse carriage along the Nile to the huge temple complex of Karnak, located just north of the city on the east side of the river. One could easily spend days there, but a morning was all we had. Added to by various Pharaohs over the centuries, Karnak sprawls out over sixty acres, some of which is yet unexplored. The largest and most ancient part is the Temple of Ammon, where we strolled with wonder through the Great Hypostyle Hall. There 134 giant columns, all ornately decorated with hieroglyphics, stand in an area as large as a football field. A sacred lake, a giant banquet hall, obelisks, rows of sphinx statues (crouching creatures with human heads and animal bodies), and towering, thick walls, all in various stages of ruin, seemed to go on endlessly.

One evening we and our friends went by "falucca" for a sail on the Nile. Gracefully shaped Egyptian sailboats originally used as work boats, faluccas are hand crafted and colorfully painted. Our white-robed skipper, "Tarzan", told of how he had helped his grandfather haul materials down the river by falucca. Now they take tourists, some as far as the Aswan Dam, two-hundred miles to the south. After sunset a full moon rose, and we glided back to the shore. The skipper's helper climbed to the top of the mast to gather the large sail in, skillfully wrapping and tieing it as he came down.

Near our small hotel, which overlooked the Nile, stood the ruins of Luxor Temple, smaller than Karnak but still grand, covering several city blocks. Lit up at night, it was a glorious reminder of the past.

After two days in Luxor we were back on board COR-MORANT, headed 250 miles north along the Gulf of Suez to Port Suez and the Suez Canal. From Port Suez we would visit Cairo and the last remaining Wonder of the Ancient World...the Pyramids of Giza.

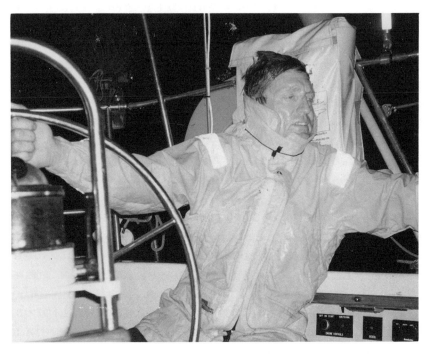

Rough weather in the Gulf of Suez

A HARROWING JOURNEY IN THE GULF OF SUEZ
(Foul weather, civil war, and a fatal fire at sea)

We sailed north from Safaga on a brisk, sunny day to Hurghada and on towards the Gulf of Suez. We had no idea the trip to Port Suez, which should have been a four or five day passage, would take us two weeks, the most difficult two weeks of our entire sail around the world.

At Hurghada we anchored in front of the Sheraton Hotel and dinghied ashore, where we checked for mail and had a delicious and inexpensive Egyptian dinner with Dixon and Sonia from RIVA. We set sail at dawn on a fresh breeze, intending to cross the forty miles of the Straits of Gubal to anchor off the southern tip of the Sinai Peninsula at Sharm el Sheik.

At the half-way point the winds had increased to 35 knots and were now on the nose; we had to turn back. With the wind behind us we practically surfed the twenty miles back to anchor in the shelter of Gifatin Island, near Hurghada. Here we waited four days for a break in the weather.

The Red Sea and Gulf of Suez were taking their toll on our fleet of more than sixty sailboats going north that year. During the four days we waited at Gifatin Island we were joined by six other boats, while others up and down the Red Sea were having significant troubles.

PHILMAR, a British boat riding at anchor at Safaga while her owners were inland at Luxor, broke her anchor chain. The 35-knot winds and current quickly swept the 26-foot boat towards a reef. She was saved only by the quick action of observant yachtsmen who, in their dinghies, held her off the reef until a large dive boat could tow her to a safe mooring.

Alan, a seventy-four year old British single handler

with whom we had dinner in Aden, lost his 32-foot wooden boat on a reef approaching Port Sudan. He had gone below to check his position on the chart, but strong winds and current swept him onto the reef he was passing. He was saved, but his home of twenty years was a total loss.

Phil, a young Australian single hander on TARAKAI whom we had met in Thailand, had insurmountable engine problems and put into the North Yemenese port of Al Mukha just as civil war broke out. After enduring the bombing and strafing of the city for five days, he was able to find a cargo ship leaving port to carry him and his 22-foot boat to England, where he would make repairs.

Two other friends had their dinghies stolen from different beaches while they were ashore in Egypt, and one Swiss boat ran aground in 35-knot winds and high seas. The boat was saved when the skipper agreed to pay an Egyptian fishing boat $400 cash to tow him to deep water. When more money was demanded and the fishing boat crew started to overpower him and his family and take items off the boat, our Swiss friend pulled out a hidden pistol, fired it into the air, and the fishing boat fled. Such things are rare, but they do happen in the Gulf of Suez.

When the weather finally broke for a day we raced thirty miles north along the Egyptian coast to anchor in Endeavor Bay. Four other boats joined us as the weather quickly deteriorated, and again we had to wait at anchor. To our front lay the Straits of Gubal, where the Gulf of Aqaba, the Gulf of Suez and the Red Sea meet.

Here the U.S. Navy was interdicting commercial shipping, checking for U.N. embargoed goods going to or from Iraq through Jordanian ports. By monitoring the maritime radio, we had a front row seat to this ongoing drama. Some of what we were to see and hear in the next twelve hours would leave an indelible imprint on us.

At midnight, unknown to us, a fire ignited in the engine room of a large passenger ship steaming north eight miles away from our anchorage. On board were more than six hundred Arabs returning from their pilgrimage to Mecca. High winds quickly spread the fire and within minutes the ship was engulfed. "MAYDAY" was called as the Egyptian captain directed the passengers and crew to abandon ship. A U.S. Navy warship (USS Briscoe—#977) responded immediately and took control of the rescue effort.

Four oil-rig supply vessels, a cruise ship, a container ship and a passing American yacht, HIGH C's (a 60-foot motorsailer in whose company we had been sailing periodically during the past year) were all on the scene within the hour. HIGH C's rescued twenty-two people after they jumped into the rough waters to escape the flames.

By dawn, a remarkable rescue had been accomplished in very difficult circumstances, with over 560 people saved. Of the approximately 40 losses, two were babies born in lifeboats.

The remains of the burning hulk, now adrift, passed three miles in front of our anchorage, and we watched in stunned silence as the smoking form just disappeared in a vapor cloud. Sea water had rushed in past the red-hot buckling plates of the hull, sending the ship to the bottom.

Another break in the weather allowed us to sail for twenty-six hours, making 110 miles before the wind again howled and the seas became too rough. We put in to the desolate harbor of Abu Zenima on the Sinai coast to wait for yet another break in the weather.

Twice we tried to leave in the early morning hours but were turned back by strong north winds and heavy seas. Finally we were able to make it fifteen miles to the next anchorage by hugging the coast, where towering cliffs of the Sinai gave us some protection from wind and wave.

At Ras Mal'ab, a low lying sand peninsula, we found shelter from the seas, but not from the roaring wind which was now loaded with stinging sand from the Sinai desert. Our teeth were gritty with fine sand and CORMORANT took on a distinctly reddish glow about her decks and rigging.

The weather again eased, allowing us to move north yet another thirty miles along the Sinai coast to El Sudr. After a sleepless night, where strong currents and high winds caused us to drag our anchor twice, we finally crept the remaining twenty-two miles to the Port Suez Yacht Club.

With the treacherous Red Sea and Gulf of Suez finally behind us, we relished being in the calm winds and quiet waters at our mooring on the edge of the Suez Canal. There we caught our breath and enjoyed watching the steady stream of passing ships, as we prepared for our turn to transit the Suez Canal.

CAIRO AND THE SUEZ CANAL
(We visit the Pyramids by camel)

Once CORMORANT was securely moored at the Suez Yacht Club after our arduous trip up the Red Sea, we set off to see nearby Cairo and the Pyramids. Along with Jack and Heather from WIRRAWAY, we boarded a crowded public bus in the cool of the morning for the two-hour trip.

Cairo is located at the base of the Nile Delta, and most of Egypt's population lives in this teeming metropolis or along the narrow Nile Valley, stretching to the south.

Finding a place to stay was not a problem. As in Luxor, terrorist scares had kept the tourists away from Cairo, but we felt completely safe. In fact, we were greeted in a friendly way by strangers on the streets. "Welcome", we heard, over and over again.

The Pyramids are just across the Nile from Cairo, to the west. Our taxi driver took us to a side entrance, where we bargained for two camels and two horses to ride. A guide named Kimo came along with us, saying we "just had to make him happy" (in other words, he wanted a good tip). We began our two hour ride with Ward and Heather on the camels and Judy and Jack on horseback. Young boys led the animals.

Leaving a strip of souvenir booths behind, we felt transported back over 4,000-years as we made our way carefully down the narrow path. Soon we could see in the distance, across a rolling plain of sand, the imposing sight of six pyramids. In the foreground was the Great Sphinx, a colossal statue of a crouching lion with a human head.

The Great Pyramid of Cheops, the largest of the pyramids, stands forty-stories high and covers an area larger than five football fields. Built in the time of the Old Kingdom, it is said to be the last remaining of the Seven Wonders of the Ancient World.

Huge stone building blocks, each more than thirty feet long, were mined in faraway hills and ferried down the Nile. They were then dragged to the site along a track which took as long to construct as the Pyramid itself....more than ten years. According to Kimo, the hundreds of thousands of slaves who built the Pyramids were subsequently put to death, so that the layout of the interior burial chambers could be kept secret.

The two other large pyramids are those of Chephren and Mycerinus. The three smaller ones are "satellites" to Mycerinus', dedicated to his queens. They are all funerary monuments. Built to mind-boggling mathematical perfection, the large pyramids were placed in a diagonal line, so that no one blocks the sun from the other two. A red sun was just setting behind the Pyramids as we made our way back to the starting point, having traded off on the horses and camels midway through our journey back in time.

Bright and early the next morning we were off to the Egyptian Museum in Cairo, which houses one of the greatest collections of ancient treasures in the world. We saw the contents of tombs we had seen earlier in the Valley of the Kings near Luxor, principally the funerary treasury of King Tutankhamen. Rows of elaborately decorated golden beds, chairs, tables, and carriages dazzled our eyes, and there were rooms full of glittering jewels and other personal objects. There were gold replicas of "King Tut's" face, and molds to fit in layers over his mummified body. These would be placed in a series of elaborate burial chambers, constructed to fit inside one another.

Towering statues seemed to keep watch over all the mummies, ancient wall paintings, delicate papyrus, and carved objects depicting life in ancient Egypt. The oldest item there is the Narmer *stele*, a perfectly preserved five thousand year old slate tablet. It would take weeks to see all that is in the Egyptian Museum; unfortunately we had just one day.

We rode the clean, modern subway to the Citadel, the oldest section of the city, where we toured the Coptic Museum. Located in an old Coptic, or Egyptian Christian church, it houses precious icons, sacred works of art dating back to 500 A.D.

*   *   *   *   *

Back on board CORMORANT, we quickly made preparations for our transit of the Suez Canal. Our agent, The Prince of the Red Sea, had made most of the arrangements while we were in Cairo, and so in less than a week from our arrival at Port Suez we began our two-day trip through the canal.

This vital waterway was completed in 1869 by French engineer Ferdinand de Lesseps, who supervised the work of more than 25,000 Egyptian laborers. They moved more than ninety-seven million cubic yards of earth to link three lakes and create this hundred-mile long Canal which saves thousands of sea miles between the Mediterranean Sea and the Indian Ocean. The canal was enlarged in the 1980's to accommodate modern-day supertankers.

Sailboats begin their two day journey north after the faster northbound convoy of large ships. We were joined by Abdul, our pilot for the first day, who immediately offered to steer CORMORANT down the straight "ditch". Unlike the Panama Canal, the Suez Canal has no locks, only flat, unending sand on both sides. In its history the Suez Canal has been closed three times, most recently from 1967 until 1974. Remnants of the 1967 Six Day War with Israel still littered the sand dunes.

We anchored for the night near the city of Ismailia, and at dawn welcomed Ahmed, our pilot for the second day. After passing close to oncoming giant ships from the world over, we continued our solitary motoring past only sand dunes, an occasional Army post, or an isolated goat herd cooling off in the refreshing waters of the canal.

At Port Said, the northern end of the Suez Canal, Ahmed left us by way of a pilot boat that came alongside, after receiving his customary "gift" ($5.00, an amount all yachts had agreed to as the tip for the pilot). The crew of the pilot boat and of a police boat asked for "gifts" of cigarettes or beer, but we politely refused.

Once clear of the breakwater we raised our sails and headed into the blue Mediterranean Sea. We were anxious to reach Cyprus, a two day sail away, and our first taste of Western culture since leaving Australia seven months earlier.

CYPRUS OFFERS A MUCH-WELCOMED CHANGE
(Friendly people make island a delight)

Exiting the Suez Canal we headed for Cyprus, a brisk forty- hour sail north across the sparkling blue Mediterranean Sea. Our Red Sea sailing companions on RACONTEUR III and RIVA remained at anchor off Port Said harbor; they would sail to Israel the following day.

It had been seven months since we left Australia, and Larnaca, Cyprus was the first port where things looked "normal" to our western eyes. After months of covering up our arms and legs in Muslim countries, here we saw people in shorts and tank tops strolling the sidewalks. Shops, restaurants, ship chandlers, grocery stores, pizza, ice cream, laundromats, modern taxis, a clean, efficient post office, local buses that ran on time, and especially the friendly people made Cyprus a delight.

Cyprus became an independent nation in 1960, only to have its northern third annexed by Turkey in 1974. A bitter hatred exists between the Cypriots in the south (ethnically associated with Greece) and the Turks, who continue to occupy the northern portion of this now divided country.

Alongside the dock at Larnaca Marina we spent hours cleaning reddish grit and encrusted salt off the boat, enjoying the unlimited supply of fresh, clean, drinkable water. This was our first time in a fully-equipped marina in 18-months, and it was here that most of our cruising friends gathered after following a variety of routes and schedules coming up the Red Sea.

After just five days in Cyprus we left for the island of Rhodes, Greece to keep a long-standing date with friends arriving from the U.S. On the day that we headed south out of Larnaca a fresh breeze grew to 30 knots on the nose. After six hours of hard motor-sailing we had only gone six miles, but we were finally able to round a point and, putting the wind on our beam, headed for Rhodes, a four-day sail to the northwest.

Suez Canal, May, 1994

Lobsterman and his catch
Sudan, Red Sea

CORMORANT at anchor in Suakin

Hedley and "Tarzan" on a falucca ride
Nile River, Luxor, Egypt

At the Pyramids with Jack and Heather Willliams of WIRRAWAY

CYPRUS TO ITALY

"Somehow, almost as if He is nodding, Greece still remains under the protection of the Creator. Men may go about their puny, ineffectual bedevilment, even in Greece, but God's magic is still at work and, no matter what the race of man may do or not do, Greece is still a sacred precinct and my belief is it will remain so until the end of time."

From : "The Colossus of Maroussi"
by Henry Miller (Written in 1941)

ON TO RHODES
(An island rich in history, strategically located)

They say you either love Rhodes or you hate it. We loved it, particularly busy Mandraki Harbor on the northern tip of the island. Rhodes is the hub for air and sea transportation in the western Mediterranean, and we soon discovered that ports in Turkey, Cyprus, Israel and Egypt are easily reached by ferryboat or hydrofoil. Measuring roughly fifty by twenty miles, Rhodes ("Rodos" to the Greeks) is the largest of the Dodecanese chain, the string of twelve sun-drenched Greek isles lying just off the western coast of Turkey.

After recent visits to the many xenophobic Arab countries along our path, being with the Greek people was like being with family. In fact, we learned that many Greeks have dual citizenship with the U.S. We found the Greeks on Rhodes to be warm and friendly; fun-loving, yet feisty and staunchly independent.

During its golden era (5th through 3rd Centuries B.C.), strategically located. Rhodes was the political, commercial, and religious center for the entire region. In 305 B.C. Rhodes withstood a year-long attack which included the use of an immense siege tower nine stories high. In recognition of the Rhodians' bravery, the gigantic Colossus of Rhodes was built. One of the Seven Wonders of the Ancient World, this huge bronze statue of the sun god, Helios, supposedly straddled the harbor entrance until it was toppled by an earthquake in 227 B.C.

Rhodes' past is most apparent in the prominent castle built during the Crusades by the Knights of the Order of St. John when they ruled the island from 1309 to 1522. In the months to come we would visit many of their smaller castles built along the sea routes to Jerusalem from the West. It was from these fortresses that the

Knights would venture forth with "a cross in one hand and a sword in the other", in defense of Christendom.

Much of pulse of the city beats behind the castle's four miles of massive perimeter walls. The main palace of the "Grand Master" of the Knights, refurbished during World War II by the occupying Italians as a future home for Mussolini, is an exquisite medieval showpiece.

Thousands of tourists are disgorged daily from cruise ships and ferryboats to crowd the colorful shopping streets and roam the castle. One day while we were at anchor off the rock jetty of Rhodes Harbor we counted fourteen large ships tied to the small commercial wharf to our front. Many of these had passed within fifty yards of CORMORANT to drop their anchor and then expertly swing their stern to the quay. Even the ill-famed and ill-fated cruise ship ACHILLE LAURO docked off our bow in Rhodes. Though Rhodes has been under the rule of Turks, Italians, and Greeks over the years, it still maintains much of its own individuality, largely as a result of the Knights of St. John era. Rhodes is unlike any other Greek isle we visited, and is fully deserving of its unique reputation.

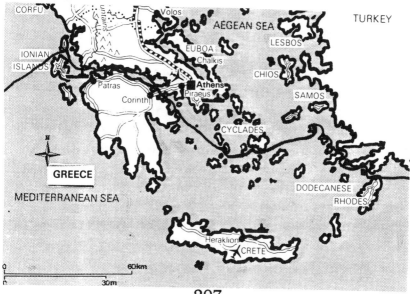

SAILING THE DODECANESE ISLANDS
(Sleepy towns, churches, castles and sheep)

Leaving Rhodes on a brisk westerly breeze, we set out to explore the rest of the Dodecanese chain of Greek isles. Lying to the northwest of Rhodes, these twelve islands are almost all within view of the meandering Turkish coastline, offering us nightly anchorages in the sparkling Aegean Sea.

With our friends George and Roberta Vest from Georgia on board, our first stop was Simi, a tiny island tucked between two westward-extending peninsulas of Turkey. Less than ten miles in diameter, this ink splat-shaped island offered delightful anchorages at every twist and turn. We would return here three more times while cruising in the Aegean Sea.

Tacking once in order to round a jutting arm of Turkey, we were anchored by early afternoon in quiet Pethy harbor by a tiny fishing village. The following morning we motored past sheep grazing on steep, brown hillsides around a bend to Simi Town, a bustling little u-shaped harbor tucked inside a broad bay.

Here sailboats were tied to the quay "stern to", known as "Med-mooring", a technique we were soon to master. Dropping anchor, we backed towards the empty space between two boats, throwing lines ashore to Mike, the dockmaster. We then tightened our anchor chain to keep us far enough off the dock to avoid hitting it, but close enough to step ashore. It took the coordination of all four of us. Mike never uttered a word, but from his gestures and expressions, all made with a cigarette dangling from his mouth, we knew what he wanted.

Simi is renowned for its classic architecture and brightly colored houses, which rise sharply from the water's edge and crowd the hills on three sides. Hiking in broiling sunlight to the top along a twisting walkway with narrow steps, we wound past homes and shops, wondering how furniture or even groceries get to where no vehicles can go.

Our reward was a breathtaking view of the harbor below and lunch at a shady *taverna*, where we got our first taste of Greek salad and *stifado*, a succulent beef stew. As darkness fell Simi Town looked like a fairyland, with street lights dotting the hillsides and reflecting off the water.

The following day we motored fifty-five miles over glassy seas to an anchorage along the southern coast of the Bodrum Peninsula of Turkey. We then headed for Kalimnos, our next stop in the Dodecanese. With a crosswind to contend with, "Med-mooring" was more difficult here, but we were ready to walk the town by 2:00 p.m., only to find that everything shuts down, even the traffic, until 5:00p.m.!

Ward was able to arrange for fuel delivery the following morning, and for the first time since leaving Singapore seven months earlier we took on diesel from a fuel hose instead of jugs. That alone made Kalimnos worth visiting, but we also enjoyed a sunset dinner on the far side of the island, and visiting a museum in the former home of a wealthy Greek sponge trader.

Kalimnos is known as the "sponge capital of the world". Divers used to go down as far as ninety feet to bring up those unusual organisms, but now more modern methods employ nets. The real sponges are sold mainly to tourists, with synthetic sponges fulfilling most of the world's needs.

We left this busy, working harbor and headed for the island which was to be our favorite....Leros, a half-day sail away. Just one other sailboat joined us in picturesque Paneli Harbor, which is overlooked by a huge medieval castle high on a hill. Three tavernas dotted the shoreline, and small fishing boats chugged past us at dawn and dusk.

Leros is a favorite of British and German tourists, but the large cruise ships do not stop there. Weekly ferries from Athens and daily hydrofoils that ply the Dodecanese waters stop at the main harbors of Laki and Agia Marina. There are no fancy resort hotels, just small rooming houses in sleepy towns. The rolling countryside is dotted with churches and an occasional ruin, and the castle that loomed over our quiet anchorage.

On another stop at Leros, with Linda and Jauncey Sweet from Fredericksburg on board, we rented motorscooters and rode from one end of the island to the other. We stopped at the ruins of the Temple of Artemis and also at the Church of St. Isadore, the only structure on a rocky islet reached by a foot path, which is covered by the sea at high tide.

Following the steep, winding road up to the castle, we could see CORMORANT, looking like a toy far below. Picnicking at the castle, swimming in the harbor at the end of a hot, exhausting day, and leisurely, inexpensive but sumptuous dinners in the tavernas gave us lasting memories of Leros.

Perhaps the most well known of the Dodecanese Islands, besides Rhodes, is Patmos. It was while imprisoned in a cave on Patmos in the year 96 A.D. that St. John the Theologian wrote the Apocalypse, found in the Book of Revelation in the Bible. The cave is preserved as part of an underground Greek Orthodox church, and is visited by millions every year.

We visited Patmos, known to the Greeks as the "Sacred Island", three times while sailing in the Dodecanese Islands. Anchoring in the harbor or "Med-mooring" at the quay, we would hike halfway up the hill to the cave, where we attended services in the sacred Grotto. We filed past the silver-trimmed cracks in the rock wall along with reverent Greeks who paused and kissed these holy places through which God spoke to St. John. Dozens of elderly, black-clad Greek women did not let the many steps down into the Grotto deter them, and they made us feel welcome, offering cake and coffee as we exited.

Continuing up the narrow path to the summit, we reached the Monastery of St. John the Theologian. Perched on the highest hill of Patmos, this massive structure broods over the entire island, and can be seen from miles away at sea. Erected in 1088 A.D., it is still in use. As we roamed the cavernous halls and courtyards, we could see monks carrying out their daily routine.

Leaving Patmos our final time, we anchored overnight at the island of Lipsi with Jack and Joyce Munsey from Annapolis on board. We then sailed overnight down the Dodecanese Island chain to Simi, then Rhodes. The seasonal northwest wind blew us gently past Leros and Kalimnos. Just after midnight as we were rounding the Turkish mainland, the wind funnelled through the mountains and roared down on us at 40 knots. We scurried to get the jib in, and were glad that we had reefed the mainsail at dusk.

At dawn we rounded Simi and tucked in to an idyllic anchorage at the south end of the island, only to be chased around to the west later in the day as the wind shifted to the south and increased. Along with several other boats we sought shelter in the protected inner bay at Panormiti.

There, with a monastery by the water's edge and steep mountains all around, a full moon shone on the still waters as we enjoyed our last night with the Munseys. They would fly home from Rhodes and we would sail east to Marmaris, Turkey.

EXPLORING INLAND TURKEY
(Ruins, rugs, and hot sulfur baths)

The incessant beat of music from the all-night disco ceased just moments before the wailing of the Muslim early-morning call to worship began. Both sounds wafted across the waters to our anchorage in Bodrum, Turkey. In this country, East meets West, old customs confront new, and the people are as friendly and honest as any we have met on our journey.

*　　*　　*　　*　　*

On arriving in Turkey, we pulled into the glitzy, modern Netsel Marina in the ancient town of Marmaris. It was the first of many marinas we would visit in the Mediterranean, and it felt like pure luxury to have electricity and water right at the dock. This marina even provided sumptuous bathroom facilities.

Here we left CORMORANT while we took a three-day excursion by rental car. Accompanied by Linda and Jauncey Sweet, we set off into the Turkish interior.

In Marmaris, as in Bodrum, a medieval castle guards the shoreline of the busy harbor, and a maze of narrow streets, many just for pedestrians, contains endless open markets and shops. Once outside the marina and the more modern sections of Marmaris, we drove on narrow, hilly roads, passing an occasional oxcart loaded down with cotton, and colorfully dressed laborers bending over crops in the fields.

We decided to stop for lunch at a small, family-owned restaurant along the Datca peninsula. After much discussion and being shown some frozen fish, we settled on chicken, presuming it was already stewing in a pot we could see on the stove. Soon, seated at our outdoor table, we heard loud squawking noises and saw two chickens being chased through the garden by the cook and two small boys. Suddenly it registered; they were catching our lunch! Protesting emphatically, we immediately changed our order to soup and rice.

The friendly owner, eager to improve his English, sat down to chat with us while we ate. A box on the counter for tips had written on it: "We love you." and "The customer is always right."

Still faced with a three-hour drive, we headed east over the mountains. Our destination was Pamukkale, where mineral deposits resembling ice and snow cover huge cliffs, and healing water from hot springs fills pools that have been enjoyed since ancient days.

Just outside our hotel room, which was in a garden setting, toppled Roman columns lay strewn across the bottom of a shallow swimming pool. We luxuriated in the bubbly, warm waters that evening and again before breakfast. Ruins of the ancient city of Hieropolis lay behind natural pools at the top of the cliffs, and Turkish families still come here in great numbers to wade in the soothing waters.

Another three-hour drive to the northwest took us to Ephesus, understandably the most visited attraction on the Turkish mainland. We joined crowds of tourists, many of then Americans from cruise ships, to walk the length of this former hillside city. Most impressive were the reconstructed three-story facade of the Library of Celsus, and the giant amphitheater where Paul preached. We roamed past ornate arches, statues, and parts of buildings more than two-thousand years old.

The adjacent modern-day town of Selcuk boasts the Basilica of St. John, built in the sixth century on the site of the apostle's tomb. On a nearby hilltop is a small house called Meryemana, where some believe the Virgin Mary spent her last days and was buried.

Meandering down the coast, we stayed overnight in

the busy, modern port of Kusadasi, finding moderately priced rooms with no difficulty. We walked through Priene, a former seacoast town now silted in by years of receding waters, as is Ephesus. Practically the only visitors there, we freely roamed the ancient streets, which are laid out in a perfect grid.

Miletus, farther along our way, has a large, well-preserved amphitheater. We stopped for a tasty, reasonably priced buffet lunch in Didyma, where ruins of a colossal temple to Apollo stand in the center of town. The famed Head of Medusa, crowned with snakes for hair, is there in the courtyard.

We stopped at a carpet farm, where colorful handwoven carpets were laid out to dry over acres of land. Turkish women and girls labor at looms night and day, and we were told that some of the smallest carpets, those with the most knots tied per inch by the tiniest hands, go for the highest prices. Young Turkish girls weave the rugs to provide for their dowry.

*   *   *   *   *

We again left CORMORANT at the dock in Marmaris and took a hydrofoil shuttle to Rhodes, Greece. There we and the Sweets boarded a large ferryboat for the two-day trip to Israel, where we would visit the Holy Land for ten days. Ferries are an easy and inexpensive way to get around the Eastern Mediterranean. They offer a choice of accommodations from hard benches to private cabins, with a mix of local people and tourists, mostly backpackers, on board.

A SIDE TRIP TO ISRAEL
(Holy sites are awe-inspiring)

Arriving at the seaport of Haifa, Israel we found ourselves in the midst of a full-fledged bomb scare. We had just joined the line at Customs in the port building when a garbled loudspeaker announcement had people muttering as they hurried outside. We followed and learned that a "bomb" had been found in luggage being screened in a separate room. Soon the owner identified the metallic object as a radio, not a bomb, and we were back in line waiting to officially enter this historic land.

*   *   *   *   *

Instead of taking an organized tour, we took one of the frequent public buses for the two-hour trip to Jerusalem. Soldiers on weekend pass, with weapons slung over their shoulders, crowded our bus; they are a common sight throughout Israel.

As soon as we arrived in the Jerusalem bus station another bomb scare sent us scurrying. We waited for the "all clear" and then, lugging all our bags, the four of us caught a city bus to the walls of Old Jerusalem.

We found Christ Church Guest House just inside the Jaffa gate. The 150-year old compound, which used to house the British Embassy, now serves as an Anglican church and hostel, an outpost of Christianity that became our home and refuge for the four days we spent in this intriguing city.

The tiny, twisting streets of Old Jerusalem and the hundreds of cubbyhole shops that line them took us back in time. Often a donkey would pass us as we wove our way along the Via Dolorosa. We visited each of the stations of Jesus' fateful journey to his crucifixion 2,000-

215

years ago. Hawkers blurred the atmosphere, but they weren't pushy. They know that pilgrims to these sacred places need some serenity to sense the way it must have been.

The Garden Tomb, located just outside the Damascus Gate, best conveyed the natural and spiritual environment to us. Inside the Church of the Holy Sepulcher, the traditional site of Christ's tomb, we had crowded shoulder to shoulder with a dozen other visitors. In the Garden Tomb we could be alone. Linda captured our thoughts best when she emerged from five minutes in the tomb and said, "You know, the most magnificent thing is that He is not here. He is risen!"

We traced other biblical sites: the birthplace of Christ in nearby Bethlehem, the Garden of Gethsemane with its gnarled trees, the stark and arid Kidron valley below the city, and the Mount of Olives....now used as a cemetery. Being in these holy places was awe-inspiring, and we became convinced that a trip to Israel is a must for all Christians.

Jerusalem is also of great significance to the Jewish and Islamic faiths, and we found it comforting that these three great religions coexist within the walls of Old Jerusalem.

We joined hundreds of Jews at the Western ("Wailing") Wall and added our written prayers to the thousands stuffed in the cracks of the wall. We then climbed up to visit the nearby Muslim Dome of the Rock.

Outside the walls of Old Jerusalem, broad streets and modern shopping areas reminded us that this is a present-day capital city. The sight of two soldiers, male and female, holding hands, weapons slung over their shoulders, reflected the awkward harmony of today's Israel.

*   *   *   *   *

One day we rode a crowded "share taxi" to Jericho, an hour to the east. Halfway there the taxi pulled off the road to let an older woman off. We watched as she followed a rocky path to her home, a makeshift Bedouin tent in the scruffy hills adjacent to the roadway.

Jericho was built around a lush oasis in the harsh land near the Jordan River. We visited soon after the Palestinians gained control of this predominantly Arab town in the West Bank, and found great happiness and a sense of hope among the people we met.

We walked the tumbledown walls of Old Jericho, then took a taxi ten miles south to the Dead Sea, where we swam with remarkable buoyancy. The sea is an acrid mixture of water from the Jordan River and minerals leached from the surrounding land. Unwittingly we went underwater and opened our eyes. We both felt blinded for ten minutes by the stinging chemicals. Every open cut and bruise we had was gone the next day, healed by the medicinal waters of the Dead Sea.

By public bus we travelled to Tiberius, sixty miles to the north along the shores of the Sea of Galilee. The sea is really a large lake, with the Golan Heights rising from its eastern shore. Israel has occupied this part of Syria since 1967.

We found rooms at the Church of Scotland Center and rented a car to see more. Driving the hills of the Golan we were impressed by the rolling country and lack of settlements in this open land. The dichotomy of the quiet hills in the distance, and the throb of the resort town of Tiberius, seemed to typify what is Israel.

Later, as we waded in the Jordan River beside the barbed-wire fence and minefields that separate Israel from Jordan, a jeep patrol of friendly, armed Israeli soldiers stopped to talk. Spirits were high and tensions relaxed because of recent successes in the peace process between Israel and Jordan.

But our main purpose in Galilee was to walk where

Christ walked. In Nazareth we drank from the well where Mary first learned she would bear the Christ child, and then we walked the streets of Jesus' youth. Now a bustling little city, Nazareth still gave us the feeling that we were in Christ's hometown.

Travelling around the shore of the Sea of Galilee we stopped where Jesus fed five thousand people with five loaves of bread and two fish. We visited the Mount of Beatitudes, the ruins of Capernaum, where much of Jesus' ministry was carried out, and Peter's home by the sea.

Having seen, touched and walked among the humble sites in Galilee, we realized that Jesus' impact on the world defies human understanding. A dozen simple fishermen, tax collectors, and carpenters from this tiny region changed mankind forever.

*　　*　　*　　*　　*

We parted with the Sweets at the Sea of Galilee; they headed back to Fredericksburg and we returned by ferryboat to Rhodes and then the short hop by hydrofoil to Marmaris, Turkey where CORMORANT was waiting.

TURKEY'S TURQUOISE COAST LIVES UP TO NAME
(By water to the rock tombs)

Our guidebook for cruising in Turkish waters was aptly called "The Turquoise Coast of Turkey." It is no wonder that hundreds of tourists, mostly Europeans, come each year to the coastal cities to charter the large, graceful wooden sailboats called "gulets". We often found ourselves anchored next to one of these boats, which come with a skipper and a crew and provide lavish meals. Most never raise their sails, if they even have them, going everywhere by motor instead.

Doc and Peggy Bahnsen from Yorktown, Virginia joined us for a five-day cruise along the Turkish coast. After a leisurely sail each day, we would anchor in a picturesque lagoon and snorkel over ancient ruins in the clear water, sometimes rowing ashore for dinner in a rustic, secluded restaurant.

One day we arranged for a trip up the Koycegiz River in a small motor launch, winding through narrow twists and turns in the marshes. We stopped to hike up a hill to the ruins of a silted-in city that dated back to 900 BC.

Farther upstream we passed the ancient Lycian Tombs, ornate facades neatly set in the mountain above us. After lunch in a small town along the river, we continued on to some sulfur baths, where we soaked in warm mud with crowds of tourists. After retracing our route back to the boat in the afternoon heat, we couldn't wait to plunge in for a cool swim.

We sailed back to Rhodes, where Doc and Peggy left us and we began our preparations to cross the Aegean Sea for the last time.

CROSSING THE AEGEAN SEA
(Dramatic Santorini is the highlight)

There are days in the Aegean Sea when the cloudless sky and the calm waters blend in an uninterrupted vista of blue. Rocky islands dot the scene, their whitewashed villages cascading down hillsides like icing on a cake. And on almost every crest, a solitary church stands silhouetted against the sky. This is the Aegean, rich in the myths of antiquity and a colorful, often chaotic, history.

*　　*　　*　　*　　*

We had spent a month working hard to prepare COR-MORANT for this last year of our sail around the world. At Yat Lift, a boat yard near Bodrum, Turkey, we painted her bottom, scrubbed her top-sides, repaired her pumps, installed a new prop shaft and fiberglassed and painted PING, our dinghy. Living in a Turkish boat yard is an experience in itself, but for us it was fun and productive. We loved Turkey, and believe the people are the most honest we have met. The prices are still wonderful, where a good meal for two in a local restaurant can be as little as $10.00.

*　　*　　*　　*　　*

Between the Dodecanese Islands near the Turkish coast and the Greek mainland to the west, the Cyclades (pronounced "kick-la-days") Islands stretch for nearly two hundred miles. During the two summers we spent in this area we crossed the Aegean Sea three times, some of our island stops by prior plan and some hastily arranged.

A menacing northwest wind, the Meltemi, blows in

these waters in July and August. Perfectly calm periods can be punctuated with up to five days of strong blows as high as 40 knots, often gusting higher in otherwise serene anchorages.

Taking refuge in Vathy harbor on the island of Sifnos, we set a third anchor, then watched as gusts overturned dinghies and sent some smaller boats dragging across the harbor. The following day, tense crews sat in the cockpits of every boat in the harbor, as winds up to 53 knots rushed down from the mountaintop.

A year earlier, after seeing some of the sights on mainland Greece and the Peloponnese, we had set out from Poros Island, near Athens, with Linda and Jauncey Sweet on board. Our first destination was Cape Sounion, on the tip of the Attica Peninsula. A breathtaking view awaited us there, the stately ruins of the Temple of Poseidon. As we approached from the sea, it was visible for miles high above a sharp cliff. Anchoring in a quiet cove below, we hiked to the top for a close look at the weatherworn columns. British poet Lord Byron had once carved his name there, now in an area cordoned off to visitors.

Entering the Aegean the following day we encountered increasing winds, so we changed course and soon headed for nearby Seraphos. There Ward and Jauncey labored for two exhausting hours to set our anchors, finally succeeding on the fourth try. We were surprised to see Hjell and Gun on SELENA, a Norwegian boat we had met in Tahiti two years earlier, anchored nearby.

During our three-day wait there for calmer winds, we hiked to the Chora, or town center, located on a crest high above, for a magnificent view of the harbor. Seraphos is off the beaten path for tourists, with a twice weekly ferry bringing mostly Greek vacationers. A beachside taverna provided us yet another memorable Greek meal.

Soon we were off for tiny Ios, a mecca for young backpackers of all nationalities. Greek poet Homer is said to be buried there, having died at sea on a voyage from the island of Samos to Athens. We tied CORMORANT to the town quay in Ios harbor and arranged to visit magnificent and popular Santorini, southernmost of the Cyclades, by ferryboat.

Very few boats of our size go to Santorini, because of the extreme depths there. A volcanic eruption in about 1600 B.C. re-shaped this island, which is also known as Thira. Some believe it to be the long-lost Atlantis.

Our ferry entered the calm, deep waters through a pass and we could see the lonely lava rock island in the center. Rocky cliffs of the surrounding island jutted from the sea, with chalky white buildings perched high above along the crest. The road from the ferry dock wound up the sheer rock in a succession of hairpin turns.

From a cliff-edge coffee shop we could see large cruise ships directly below us, sending their passengers to the top either by cable car or by donkey, up the steep, winding path. Strolling along the crest we looked across the rooftops of residences, built into vertical slopes, and wondered how materials to build the many shops, restaurants, and hotels in this town-in-the-sky, Fira, ever got there.

Photographs of Santorini's dazzling white buildings and deep blue church domes against even bluer seas and skies adorn most Greek postcards and travel books. The geography of the island makes Santorini truly unique.

With Judy's cousin Sally Brown and her husband, Bob, with us from New Jersey for two weeks, we found two idyllic days in which to cross the Aegean, east to west. With the wind on our beam, we did a sixty-five mile day from Patmos in the Dodecanese Islands to a quiet anchorage on the southern tip of Naxos, largest of the Cyclades. The next day a similar set of sail brought us to Sifnos.

There we had a long anticipated reunion with several members of Ward's Class of 1956 from West Point. Nik Mavrotheris, B.J. and Liz O'Brien, and Harry and Jean Kotellos had chartered a 60 foot sailboat, VENEZIA, complete with captain and crew. Side by side we sailed to the nearby island of Milos the following day with extra guests on board CORMORANT. Anchoring for the afternoon at a pristine, deserted beach we enjoyed a swim and a sumptuous lunch on the VENEZIA. We had planned an excursion to the exact spot where the famous Venus de Milo statue was discovered, but bad weather forced us to cancel and move both boats to a safer anchorage.

Plagued by an elusive oil leak, much of Ward's time at anchor had been spent in the depths of the engine room. Returning to Sifnos with the Browns still on board, we got help from Brian Pearce, who had the machinery we needed on board ASTRON, his 60-foot steel trawler.

It was then that the high winds struck, and we had some tense moments when CORMORANT, helpless with engine parts disassembled, dragged anchor. With the help of our Australian friend, Jack Williams of WIRRAWAY, Brian was able to attach a line to us as we drifted by, headed for the nearby rocks. Jack also helped us get our wind generator working again, laboring all day on an inner part Ward had been unable to reach, to give us much-needed power until Ward could repair the engine.

A mechanic from the nearby landlocked town of Appolonia finally fixed our oil leak by brazing a part, which Ward carried to him. We had to put the Browns on a ferry bound for Athens, still a good day's sail away, in order to for them make their scheduled flight home.

A day after the extreme gusts ended, we set sail for the island of Poros, near Athens. We soon realized we should have given the seas another day to calm down. CORMORANT performed superbly as wave after wave doused the decks and a rogue wave broke directly on top of the bimini. We did not enjoy that ride! Relieved to be out of the windy Aegean, we began preparations to pass through the Corinth Canal and into the Ionian Sea, where the Meltemi winds don't blow.

CORMORANT alone in the Corinth Canal of Greece

NARROW SEAS, OPEN MINDS
(We transit the Corinth Canal; depart Greece)

"O.K. if we raft up with you?" we called to the Greek charter skipper watching us approach his boat. A tilt of his head, the engaging Greek acknowledgement, told us he would take our lines.

We had just arrived at the island of Poros, thirty-two miles southwest of Athens. In this crowded, popular spot, sailboats tie to each other parallel to the wall, and CORMORANT was the fifth boat out. After clambering over four bows to step ashore, we were happy when the others all departed the following day. Now, right against the wall, it was easy to take on water, fuel, groceries, and a mountain of clean laundry. We were preparing for our departure from Greece.

That afternoon we heard a friendly voice say " Ahoy, CORMORANT! May we tie to you?". A sixty-foot sailboat with a large Swiss family on board stood ready with their lines and fenders and we helped them come alongside. They immediately invited us to dinner that evening.

After a delicious meal around the huge wooden table in their cockpit, we invited all of them on board COR-MORANT. The mother and father played a duet on our electric keyboard, and all nine of them sang lively Swiss folk songs for us.

From Poros we headed for the Corinth Canal, thirty miles to our northwest, in the shadow of the remains of Ancient Corinth. Dug in the late 1800's, this three-mile-long waterway connects the Aegean and Ionian seas, saving mariners a long trip around the Peloponnese, the sprawling southern peninsula of Greece.

Approaching in the late afternoon, we radioed the canal authorities, then tied to a pier at the entrance.

fee....the most expensive three miles in the world, $150 for our 39-foot yacht. As soon as a large ship exited the canal, towed by a tug, we were given the signal to enter.

We began motoring slowly between the 250-foot high limestone cliffs that line the straight, narrow waterway. Only one-way traffic is possible, and we were the only boat going our way. Far overhead, cars and trucks rumbled over a bridge at one point, and people waved down to us from the span's walkway. Before us and in our wake stretched a spectacular ribbon of bright blue. The ancient Greeks used to drag ships across the isthmus, and we were told that the remains of the road they used can still be seen on the north side of the canal.

At the overnight anchorage we chose, a short distance beyond the canal and the modern port of Corinth, we discovered that our depth meter was not working. The wave that had doused us the week before in the Aegean had seeped through the seal and shorted out this all-important instrument. Using our small dinghy anchor tied to a line to plumb the depth, Ward was able to find a good spot to anchor that night and also the next, but we knew we could not continue using this ancient method of depth-finding.

In the Gulf of Corinth we passed beaches, vineyards, and lofty mountains. Motoring all day in stillness, we pulled in before dark to the port of Navpaktos, a tiny medieval harbor dominated by an ancient castle, whose walls wound around the hillside. Anchoring just outside the harbor, we took our dinghy in through the walled entrance for a meal ashore.

A profusion of ferry boats crossed our path the next morning at the narrowest point between mainland Greece and the Peloponnese, as we neared the Gulf of Patras. From there the waters widened and the mountains gave way to low-lying plains. Soon we were in the Ionian Sea, where the islands are lush and green, and the waters are calm compared to the lively Aegean.

are calm compared to the lively Aegean.

Scheduled to meet friends in Italy, our time to visit the Ionian Islands of Greece was limited, so we chose Ithaca, home of Homer's Odysseus, for a two-day stay. The harbor of Vathi there is said to be the finest harbor in all of Greece. Long and narrow, its anchoring depth was perfect and the picturesque town of Port Vathi stretched around the natural curve of the harbor. Ward had cleaned the depth sounder circuit board with alcohol and a cotton swab, and thankfully the instrument clicked into action just as we made our entrance.

A public bus took us up along the jagged spine of Ithaca, where we could look down to bays on each coast of this eighteen-mile long island. At the inland town of Stavros, we looked for signs of the ruins of Odysseus' castle, and were directed along a road in the noonday sun to a museum housing artifacts from the earliest times. The proprietor pointed out a spot on a nearby hill where the castle was said to have stood.

Ithaca is located on a major fault line, which may explain the disappearance of all traces of the castle. An earthquake in 1953 demolished more than half the buildings on the island. Most have been rebuilt, though crumbling remains still lie about.

We walked two kilometers down through small rocky valleys of olive trees to the tiny seaside town of Frikes. Later we moved CORMORANT to a quiet anchorage near there, where our only neighbors were two herds of goats and their keepers, who lived in makeshift huts along the beach. There is almost no flat ground on Ithaca, and we could see more goats on the rocky cliffs as we headed out the next day.

Ahead of us lay a two-day sail across the Ionian Sea. Except for some distant lightning, and a brightly lit cruise ship that passed quite close to us in the night, the crossing was uneventful, as we like it.

Judy in Santorini, Greece

Sweets and LeHardys at Wailing Wall, Jerusalem

Jauncey Sweet with Israeli soldiers on patrol
Jordan River, Israel

Temple of Apollo at Didyma, Turkey

Lycian Tombs at Dalyan, Turkey

ITALY TO MOROCCO

"Morning came with sunny pieces of cloud:
and the Sicilian coast towering pale blue in the distance.
How wonderful it must have been to Ulysses to venture into
this Mediterranean and open his eyes on all the lovliness of
the tall coasts. How marvellous to steal with his ship into
these magic harbours."

From: Sea and Sardinia
        by D.H. Lawrence

231

EXPLORING ITALY'S COAST
(Craggy scenery, active volcanoes beckon)

We arrived at the "tip of the toe" of Italy, Cape dell' Armi, where we rested at a commercial marina and cleaned the salt from CORMORANT's decks with fresh water. We were surprised to learn that Italy didn't require us to "check in", the first country we have found to be so lax. Member nations of the recently formed European Community are not subjected to the same scrutiny as are outsiders, and Italy doesn't seem to care about the few American boats that enter the country.

At nearby Reggio di Calabria three friends joined us. John and Sara Wells from California had sailed with us twice before, and Mary Gale Buchanan from Annapolis had seen us off in 1991. Now, with five on board, our 39 feet of space became very small; only good friends should try it!

Through the Straits of Messina, the narrow pass between Sicily and the Italian mainland, we experienced the same whirlpools that Homer wrote about in The Odyssey. Scilla and Charybdis still swirl at opposite sides of the northern end of the Straits, but now, with our fifty horsepower engine pushing us along, this churning waterway did not present quite the same challenge it must have for Odysseus.

Along with hundreds of Italian tourists, we lingered a few days in the Aeolian Islands just north of Sicily. The island of Volcano still has one active crater, and there we soaked in bubbling mud baths and sulphur springs just 100 yards from where CORMORANT was anchored.

After a visit to the island of Lipari, an overnight sail to the mainland took us past Stromboli Island, said to be the oldest "lighthouse" in the world. Its active volcano has guided sailors for centuries, and normally belches forth every few hours. It was quiet as we passed by, five miles offshore.

At first light Mary Gale noticed something dark in the water ahead. It was a huge whale, which allowed us to get within ten yards before slowly lifting its enormous tail in a final salute as he plunged to the depths.

Agropoli, an ancient cliff-top village, sports a large and modern harbor, where we "Med-moored" at the outer quay. We caught a public bus to walk among the ancient ruins of Paestum, eight miles away. Said to be the finest example of Greek architecture in Italy, these majestic ruins have stood for over a thousand years.

The famous Amalfi coast lured us, and after a brief cruise along Salerno beach, where U.S. Forces landed over fifty years ago, we docked at the tiny public wharf in the town of Amalfi. The tight harbor didn't allow us enough space to back in to "Med-moor". With the dockmaster yelling instructions in Italian, and CORMORANT motoring in slow, tight circles, we finally gave up and went in bow first. As he tied our bow lines, the dockmaster gave us the typical, friendly Italian shrug as if to say, "That's what I told you to do five minutes ago!"

Amalfi is a picture-postcard. From the crowded, tiny harbor and pocket beach, the terraced buildings rise up in a half circle around the water. Deep within the walls of the town, a maze of alleyways and shops greeted us, and from the central plaza wide steps led up to the magnificent "duomo", or cathedral.

We sailed along the Amalfi peninsula, with the spectacular Amalfi drive carved halfway up the cliff, pointing directly to the Isle of Capri. At Capri we docked inside the busy main harbor, then went by bus and funicular to explore this soaring rock-bound island. The view from the top of the cliff was unparalleled, with CORMORANT lying far below, ferryboats and smaller craft whizzing by.

We moved to the south side of Capri when the rolly

waters of the harbor got unbearable. As we were anchoring in thirty-foot depths a line got caught in our propeller, stopping the engine. With the wind whipping up, and the depth increasing, we drifted towards some offshore rocks. Ward dove in to cut the line away from the propeller as John laid out all 185 feet of our anchor chain. With the engine running again, we raised the anchor and moved in closer to the cliff, where we found a patch of sand only fifteen feet deep; far more suitable for anchoring.

Our crew left us in Naples, after treating CORMORANT to a berth at the Santa Lucia Marina, and us to a room at the luxurious Vesuvius Hotel, overlooking the marina and an ancient castle.

*   *   *   *   *

We sailed out of the Bay of Naples to the island of Ponza, which lay directly on our course to the northern tip of Sardinia. Nicknamed "the pearl of Rome", this popular spot off the Italian coast was overcrowded with small boats, but we anchored anyway, close to the town, in space that seemed sufficient for about ten boats. Within an hour, more than twenty boats had crowded in nearby. Fortunately the wind was calm and there were no collisions.

In mid-morning we left to make the 130-mile crossing of the Tyrrhenian Sea to Sardinia. Our passage was uneventful except during the mid-watch (midnight to three a.m.), when a spectacular lightning display danced all around us. Watching the rain-clouds on our radar, we could tell that none of them came within four miles of us. Looking around the pitch black sky we often saw six bolts of lightning strike the water simultaneously as others arched up into the night sky. God watched over us that night, as He always does, and we arrived in Sardinia unharmed.

Ward with Mary Gale Buchanan and John & Sara Wells
Aeolian Islands, Italy

A VISIT TO CORSICA, NAPOLEAN'S BIRTHPLACE
(Thrashing seas, roaring winds and a flying propeller)

A light too bright to be a star shone through the companionway into our aft bunk, waking us with a start. It was the masthead light of a boat that had been anchored nearby, now barely a foot away. We were dragging anchor in the strong wind that had suddenly come up, as were other boats in the small harbor off the town of Macinaggio, Corsica.

It was 4:30 a.m., and rather than re-anchor in the dark, Ward decided we would leave early for Livorno, Italy, a forty-five mile trip. We had planned to leave about 6:30 a.m. anyway, so our crew, Mimi and Paul Horne, could board the evening train for Paris. It would soon be daylight, and by getting a jump on the day, we thought we might even be there before lunch.

*　　*　　*　　*　　*

For a week we had been cruising the spectacular west coast of Corsica with the Hornes. We had picked them up at picturesque Bonifacio, a slit-like harbor at the south end of the island. Presided over by a walled fortress, the tiny channel and town with rows of boats and shops is totally out of view from the sea.

Then followed six idyllic days of sailing and motoring along Corsica's sheer red cliffs, quiet nights at anchor, and an occasional meal ashore for our first experience of French cuisine. On every jagged point of the meandering coastline stood a medieval lookout tower, once ready to flash signals warning of enemy approach. The further north we went, the more dramatic the scenery.

A French island, and the birthplace of Napoleon, Corsica is located closer to the Italian coast than to

France. Just to the south across Bonifacio Straits lies the Italian island of Sardinia, where we had made landfall the week before after crossing the Tyrrhenian Sea.

*   *   *   *   *

Little did we know what lay ahead as we motored out of Macinaggio that final day with the Hornes in the pre-dawn, after our anchor dragged. Once we were underway, with wind and seas behind us, there was no turning back in the gale that was developing. We had towed the dinghy all week, but soon wished it were safely lashed to the foredeck. Our wind generator, a five-foot diameter propeller mounted on a post above the stern, whirred loudly. Ward decided to wait until after dawn to stand up high on the stern pulpit to tie it down. A governor automatically stops the power flow, and it had spun in high winds before.

Suddenly a loud metallic BANG startled us. A split-second later we realized the propeller had sheared off from the pole, hit the bimini support, and broken apart. One blade hurtled through the canvas top and sliced a cockpit cushion in half, then bounced into the sea. Moments before, Paul had been in that seat, and Ward had just walked past the path of the whirling blade!

The size of the following seas had increased along with the wind, and the dinghy now planed down each huge wave, sometimes overtaking us, nearly crashing into the stern. Slightly to the south and just one-quarter of the way to Livorno lay the tiny island of Capraia. An Italian prison occupies this rocky place, where there is one small harbor. Carefully taking the waves on an angle, Ward steered towards Capraia. By 8:30 a.m. we were anchored, along with two other boats, in the flat but agitated waters of a tiny bay near the town, while the wind roared by at 40 knots.

While setting a second anchor, Ward noticed a large

237

rubber dive boat nearby. Hailing it, he arranged for Mimi and Paul to be taken to the harbor from where they could catch the last ferry to Livorno. Hastily packing, they were gone with hardly time to say good-bye, abruptly ending what was, up until that morning, a perfect week.

As long as the wind direction held us off the rocks, we felt safe where we were. Gusts up to 50 knots continued, but our anchors held. Later in the day it seemed to let up, but just before dark the two other boats in our small bay hoisted anchor, warning us that a northeast gale was expected that night. Not wanting to remain by a rocky lee shore, we followed suit, and all three boats headed for the south shore of the island of Elba, twenty-four miles away.

Thankful to be in seas and wind that nowhere matched their size and strength of that morning, we continued on until we anchored in the quiet harbor of Marino del Campo at 3:00 a.m. In more ways than one, this was surely our "longest day"!

*   *   *   *   *

Spending three days on Elba, we traveled across mountains by bus to the main harbor of Portoferraio, and visited the splendid town residence of Napoleon during his exile, the Palazzina dei Mulini. He had an even grander country home, the Villa St. Martino, which we did not see. Rested and re-supplied, we picked a quiet day to motor-sail back to Macinaggio on Corsica, where we planned to anchor for a night before heading north to Monaco.

A fresh west wind sprang up just as we reached our destination, and seeing no boats in the anchorage, we decided to berth at the large, protected marina nearby. For the next three days the wind blew, reaching a steady 50 knots for most of the afternoon, spewing foam across the harbor.

Wary skippers constantly checked lines and fenders, and we all watched when a French rescue boat, called out on emergency, towed a tiny Czechoslovakian sailboat in from a nearby rocky shoal. Two men on a jet ski had gone along to pluck a woman and child from the overcrowded, floundering boat, and were greeted with cheers as they returned safely.

The strong wind we were experiencing is called the Mistral. It blows from the west, often without notice, and we soon learned that when the Mistral arrives, all plans must be temporarily scrapped.

FREJUS, ON THE COTE D'AZUR
(Fredericksburg's Sister City gives us a royal welcome)

We had heard about Frejus, France for years, but never could have anticipated what lay ahead as we approached it along the Cote d'Azur. Learning of our trip from Phyllis Whitley, President of the Fredericksburg Sister City Association and George Van Sant, our neighbor and former Fredericksburg City Councilman, Frejus was gearing up to welcome us as celebrities.

Meanwhile, we were still slogging it out in yet another Mistral. We had crossed the Ligurian Sea from the northern tip of Corsica to Monaco. There we enjoyed a perfect day exploring the tiny principality while COR-MORANT lay tucked in a corner of Monaco harbor, home to "mega yachts" of the rich and famous.

We watched the changing of the guards at the Palace, strolled the cliff-side gardens, and spent a quiet moment at Princess Grace's grave inside the cathedral where she and Prince Rainier had been married.

But we had to move on to arrive in Frejus as planned. This Mistral had brought rain as well as strong winds, and the weather was so bad we couldn't even see Nice or Cannes as we crept along the coast. We stopped in a marina for the night to prepare CORMORANT for arrival, then scooted the remaining few miles to dock at Port Frejus at exactly 5:00 p.m.

A group of dignitaries, including the President of the Frejus "Jumelage" (Sister City Association), Gerard Ferraioli, was waiting as we backed into our reserved slip in front of the Port Captain's office. At our insistence, they all clambered aboard for a quick look at COR-MORANT, before we shared refreshments at a dockside cafe. We instantly felt like we were home among friends; such is the result of the magnificent Sister City relationship that has been building since 1980.

Elizabeth Andre would be our guide for the next few days. She endeared herself to us by her gentle effervescence and positive attitude. She ushered us into the Mayor's office where we presented a plaque from the Fredericksburg City Council, recognizing this as the first time residents of either city had traveled from one to the other by sailboat. We encouraged Frejus to sponsor someone to sail to Fredericksburg one day!

Pierre Choel, the city tour director, gave us a walking tour of Frejus and we learned more of its history as a former Roman port. Over the years Frejus had been destroyed seven times, most recently by a flood in 1959. Each time it was rebuilt, and now plans have been made to recreate an inner harbor in the same place it was during Roman rule, about a mile inland from Port Frejus.

Election Day and the annual Giant Omelette Festival occurred during the weekend we were there. Thousands turned out for the festival and Francois Leotard was re-elected Mayor of Frejus. He had been France's Minister of Defense at one time and has the charisma, ability and reputation that may propel him to higher office.

The Giant Omelette was just that. 10,000 eggs were broken, mixed, and sloshed onto an eight-foot skillet which had been placed by forklift onto a bed of coals. The "Knights of the Omelette" stirred the eggs using ten-foot wooden paddles, and then, when the eggs were done, served breakfast to about three thousand people.

The festival started with a church service where the eggs and bread were blessed, then a parade to the "kitchen" in an outdoor park. We were honored guests in the parade, and marched just ahead of the gigantic loaves of bread and the "Knights", arrayed in their huge chefs' hats. Hundreds of citizens of Frejus have visited Fredericksburg over the past sixteen years, and many asked us about people they had met there.

The warmth of our welcome continued as Elizabeth

took us to the 1,000-year old village of Roquebrune, nestled in the craggy hills nearby. We toured churches, museums, and an exquisite Italianate villa and came away impressed with this corner of the Cote d'Azur.

We enjoyed a four-hour dinner at Chez Jo with a dozen new friends from Frejus. Chez Jo started as a sidewalk pizza shop, and today, even though it is now a prominent waterfront restaurant, the owner's eighty year old mother still sells pizza from a van parked along the sidewalk.

A final meal in the home of the Deputy Mayor Michelle Guillermin and husband Jean Pierre gave us a glimpse of home life in Frejus. A delicious aroma greeted us as we stepped into their home, a 250 year old, four-story town house, with nooks and crannies everywhere. We lingered until after midnight as we knew this would be our last time with some of these new friends.

As we sailed from Port Frejus we realized how fortunate we are to know these gracious people. We echo the words from the proclamation we left in Frejus: "It is our profound hope that our two cities may continue to maintain our beautiful friendship far into the future."

*   *   *   *   *

We had a perfect sail in brisk winds and bright sunshine, past the ever-popular St. Tropez and on towards our planned anchorage near the Porquerolles Islands, the southernmost point of France on our route to the Balearic Islands of Spain. Eight miles from our anchorage at Port Man, the wind died. We turned on the motor, but within thirty minutes the wind built up again, this time to a robust 24 knots on the nose. Before we knew it, we were engulfed in yet another Mistral, this time without a cloud in the sky.

Ward crawled forward to lower all sails as the seas quickly built to twenty feet and the wind reached 50 knots. Judy steered as we struggled towards our anchorage. It took us two hours, with huge waves breaking over our bow and often with very little steerage, as the strength of wind and wave forced us into the troughs between mountains of frothing seas.

Of all the seas we have faced over the past four years, these were the most frightening, yet here we were just eight hours from Frejus and only two miles from safety. We finally rounded a point and slid into an already crowded, but flat-sea anchorage. Ward put out two anchors to hold us against the 30-knot wind as we collapsed in relief and exhaustion.

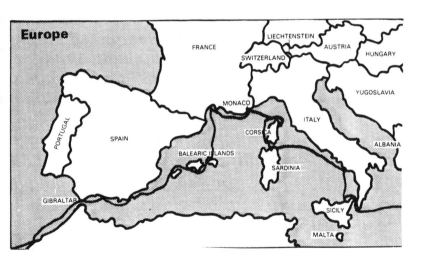

ADVENTURES IN SPAIN; ARRIVAL IN GIBRALTAR
(A frantic getaway; an injured Harbormaster)

Finally in the Western Mediterranean, we set COR-MORANT on a southwesterly course towards the Balearic Islands of Spain. We had wanted to continue along the coast to Barcelona, but that meant crossing the "Golfe du Lion", where the menacing Mistral wind are the strongest. We'd had enough of that!

Gentle winds gave us a pleasant two-day passage to the island of Menorca. At midnight we dropped anchor in Fornell harbor, using good charts, our radar, and a set of range lights on shore to guide us in.

From the sea much of Menorca looks barren, with high, rocky cliffs and an empty plain above. Ancient civilizations had left behind occasional pyramid-shaped structures. Rounding the island the next day we suddenly came upon the charming little city of Ciutadella, former capital of Menorca.

Our first night there was spent tied along a wall with other boats, near the entrance to the long, narrow harbor. We were awakened early by rolling and jostling; the wind had shifted and increased dramatically, and a huge surge was coming straight down the opening of the harbor. Our fenders were not enough to prevent the boat from rubbing and crashing against the wall.

As all boats made a frantic getaway in the early light, our metal boarding ladder caught on another boat's line, causing our stern pulpit to unseat and bend badly. Luckily the harbormaster found places for all of the sailboats deeper in the harbor among the local fishing boats, where we spent the day making temporary repairs.

When more fishing boats returned, the harbormaster found us a new place. As he helped guide us in, fending off our bow, his leg became jammed between our protruding anchor and a fixed cement post on the dock. He screamed in pain while we watched helplessly from the boat. Fishermen ashore rushed to his aid and soon he was hurried off in an ambulance.

The following day we found the hospital and visited this man, Jesus Sanchez, who had been so helpful to us. His leg was sprained, not broken, as we had feared, and he cheerfully implied that it was "all in a day's work".

While waiting for the wind to change we enjoyed this ancient city, with its tree-lined public square, quaint, narrow streets, cathedral, and fortress wall which lined the inner harbor. In the evening we walked a wide path along the cliffs to watch the daily arrival of the large inter-island ferryboat. It seemed to race through the narrow entrance and surging waters, then slowed dramatically and filled the entire inner harbor, as it made a complete turn to back into the ferry dock.

Largest of the Balearics, at about 2,000 square miles, is Mallorca. We spent ten days there in the city of Palma, tied bow-to at a large cement public pier right in the city center, along with many other cruising sailboats.

Someone has said that world cruising is repairing your engine in a series of exotic ports, and much of Ward's time in Mallorca was spent trying to solve our persistent oil leak. We did find time to visit the ancient castle high on a nearby hill, and often ambled along the broad, tree-lined boulevards to the old section of the city. The second largest Gothic cathedral in the world dominates the harbor landscape, and each evening the setting sun transformed it to a burnished gold.

The symphony hall was only a short walk from the boat, and we attended opening night of the season, with a world renown pianist and the Balearic Symphony Orchestra. Mallorca was home to artist Joan Miro, and the impressive Miro Foundation in Palma houses much of his work. Despite the oil leak, this cosmopolitan city is high on our list of favorite stops.

Human settlements in the Balearics date back to 3500 B.C. The islands have been ruled successively by the Carthaginians, the Romans, the Vandals, the Byzantine Empire, the Visigoths, and the Moors. The earliest Spanish rule was under the Catalan-Aragonese crown in 1229, and the Catalan language, a variation of Spanish, is still the official language. Located 120 miles from the Spanish mainland, their ideal climate has made the islands a popular world playground.

Sailing further south we came to Ibiza. Smaller, greener, and more cultivated, it has the same spectacular coastline as the other islands. We left CORMORANT for a few days at the Yacht Club in San Antonio Abad to visit Ward's British cousin, June LeHardy in her rustic villa which overlooks the harbor.

Ibiza Town, across the island, has a large commercial harbor overlooked by an ancient walled fortress. Judy's sister, Maude DeFrance, and her husband, Rude, joined us for a sail to the smallest and most southerly island in the Balearics, Formentera.

Low-lying and less populated, Formentera has miles of beach and bicycle paths. Emerald green waters and a sandy crescent on the nearby islet of Espalmador gave us a day of swimming and picnicking, reminiscent of times spent along the coast of Sudan in the Red Sea. After the DeFrances left us in Ibiza, we returned to Formentera and spent two days at a newly completed marina, catching up on rest and making minor repairs.

Soon we were headed southwest towards the Spanish mainland with another crew member on board, Christopher Munsey from Annapolis. We put him right to work, sharing the night watch and helping Ward reef the sails during a sudden early morning squall.

The Spanish coast is mostly rocky, brown hills, with a town here and there, where stark-white buildings stand out in contrast to the bare hills. After two nights at sea we pulled in to the marina at Aguadulce. From there we took a two and a half hour train ride through the spectacular Sierra Nevada to Grenada. The raw mountain scenery looked like a moonscape, with jagged little peaks in a barren land.

The city of Grenada lies on high ground between two mountain ranges, and contains the famous Alhambra, whose ornate Moorish palaces, courtyards, gardens, and fortress cover the area of a small town. It is beautiful beyond description. Hundreds of tourists visit there each day, to see for themselves this magical place.

In Grenada the tombs of King Ferdinand and Queen Isabella lie side by side beneath the nave of the Spanish Renaissance Cathedral.

*   *   *   *   *

Two more night anchorages along the increasingly populous Costa del Sol of Spain brought us to our next destination, Gibraltar. From a distance it looked like a snow-capped mountain rising out of the sea.

As the immense Rock, its peak shrouded in a white cloud bank, loomed ever closer, the wind swung around to the east and increased to 30 knots. We put in a triple reef, furled the jib, and rounded Gibraltar in rolly, rough conditions. Finally we were leaving the Mediterranean with all of its fluky weather.

BETWEEN THE ROCK AND A HARD PLACE
(We rest in Gibraltar and grow weary of Morocco)

After checking into Customs we tied to the visitors' dock at Sheppard's Marina, in the shadow of the Rock of Gibraltar. We chose to stay at this historic, but now seedy and out-dated yacht basin, rather than at one of the two glitzy, new marinas.

Here we ordered a new water pump from the U.S. Four days later Ward walked the half-mile to the International Airport to pick up the part and then installed it on CORMORANT, amazed at how fast things can happen in the modern world. Sheppard's was just a two-minute walk from the busy warren of shops, pubs, and restaurants of old Gibraltar, the last remnant of the British Empire in the Mediterranean.

Ownership of the Rock has changed over the centuries, with the name Gibraltar coming from a corruption of the Arabic words "Jebel Tarik" (Tarik's Mountain). Tarik was a Beber leader who landed there in 711 A.D. The Moors of North Africa occupied Gibraltar for over six centuries, and their influence is still felt. In 1462 Spain regained control, until the War of Spanish Succession (1702-1713) ended with the Treaty of Utrecht, giving Gibraltar to England "forever".

We toured the Rock and its many attractions. Natural caves, such as St. Michael's Cave, were home to the first inhabitants. Some of the more engaging current inhabitants are the "rock apes", Barbary apes who live in a semi-wild state and have as much fun watching the tourists as the tourists do watching them.

Thirty miles of man-made tunnels and roads honeycomb the Rock's interior. From many of these the British fired cannonballs down on the attacking Spanish and French fleets during the siege of 1779-1783. Though most of the town was destroyed, the British won out and have never been challenged here since, at least not militarily.

We were in Gibraltar for the twice-annual Ceremony of The Keys and also the anniversary of the Battle of Trafalgar, in which Admiral Lord Nelson was killed, and watched some of the pomp and pageantry reflecting that regal past. In both of these events the present Governor and Commander-In-Chief of Gibraltar presided, puffed up and pompous, arriving by Rolls-Royce through the shabby, decadent streets of this British outpost.

Even though modern supermarkets, office buildings and apartments are being built on newly dredged land at the waterfront, a tired air prevails throughout Gibraltar. Inside the casement walls lies the heart of the old city, where merchants of Indian, Moorish, and Spanish descent engage in commerce. Beyond the airfield, which bisects the north end of the peninsula, the Spanish border blocks the way. This was closed from 1969 to 1985, but normal relations now exist.

We left with the feeling that Gibraltar would one day belong to Spain, when England tired of pouring resources into a place whose strategic importance lay only in the past.

*   *   *   *   *

With a good wind behind us, we sailed through the Straits of Gibraltar on the outgoing current, often making 9 knots. The long swells of the Atlantic Ocean were a relief after the short, choppy seas of the Mediterranean. Once we were along the Moroccan coast and in the lee of the coast of Africa, the wind died, and we motor-sailed through the night to arrive at Mohammedia, near Casablanca, by mid-afternoon.

Information about cruising in Morocco was very limited; we were guided by a letter from an Australian couple

249

describing their sail there the year before. As we pulled into the small commercial port of Mohammedia, it was a relief to see a Moroccan man motioning for us to throw him our lines.

Rasheed turned out to be employed by the small Mohammedia Yacht Club, a hold-over from French Moroccan days. He became our local guide and gained our trust instantly. Two days later we left CORMORANT in his care while we took Chris Munsey to the airport in Casablanca. We then continued on by train to the ancient city of Marrakesh, deep in the Moroccan desert.

Arriving in Marrakesh without any room reservations, we relied on friendly taxi drivers for suggestions. We found a small hotel in the center of this dusty, old town.

During the day the nearby city square was a bustling market-place, but at twilight it transformed into an array of people and events. Snake charmers, dancers, Koran readings, small plays being acted out, Moroccan music, card games and fortune tellers competed for our attention.

We visited some of the ancient ruins of Moorish culture and wandered the narrow, twisting alleyways lined with shops selling everything from computers to meat. An animal head hanging up, dripping with blood, indicated the type meat for sale at each butcher shop.

At the far edge of the old city we found one of several tanneries. Fresh hides, with the fur still on them, were carted into the compound by donkeys. Young men squished the new skins with their feet while standing in large pots, up to their knees in an acrid lye mixture. The stench was almost unbearable.

After twenty-four hours in Marrakesh we were ready to leave. We probably had become a bit weary of third-world Muslim cultures, where bargaining is expected and "touts" constantly press visitors to buy their wares or use their services. Besides, we were anxious to get on with our upcoming Atlantic crossing.

Waving one last time to Rasheed, we backed out of the mooring in Mohammadia and continued down the Moroccan coast. Passing Casablanca, we spied the new Mohammed V Mosque, largest in the world, which we had walked around a few days before. Fog closed in on us for the rest of the day and night as we motored on, searching for the large commercial harbor of Jorf Lasfar.

We came within two miles of this huge, brightly lit port, described in detail in our Australian friend's letter, without being able to see it. It was to be our last rest stop before a five-day sail to the Canary Islands. Just as Ward said: "We'll have to go on; we can't enter the harbor if we can't see the entry lights," the fog miraculously lifted, and we motored in for a twelve-hour rest.

Right after Ward pulled the anchor up, ready to sail away the next morning, a boat-load of officials came to us and demanded to come aboard. We had tried in vain to contact them the night before but never got a response to our radio calls.

After a three-hour delay, filling out endless forms and answering the same questions from Immigration, Customs, Harbor Master, and Security officials, we were allowed to leave after paying the one-night harbor fee of $1.50. The open waters of the Atlantic were a great relief as we watched the African coast fade away, and pointed for the Canary Islands.

The Alhambra — Grenada, Spain

Arriving at Gibraltar

With Barbary apes on the Rock of Gibraltar

Arriving in Frejus, France

With the "Water Man" in Marrakesh. Morocco

MOROCCO TO ANNAPOLIS

"Behind him lay the gray Azores,
  Behind the Gates of Hercules;
Before him not the ghost of shores
  Before him only shoreless seas.
The good mate said: "Now must we pray,
  For lo! the very stars are gone.
Brave Admiral, speak, what shall I say?"
  "Why, say, 'Sail on! sail on! sail on!' "

From: "Columbus"
by Joaquin Miller

WHICH CAME FIRST, THE CANARIES OR THE ISLANDS
(Exploring the Canary Islands, preparing for the Atlantic)

Ever since the days of Christopher Columbus, most sailing vessels have made final preparations to cross the Atlantic Ocean in the Canary Islands of Spain. This year more than four hundred sailboats made the crossing, mostly during the month of December, when the weather is generally favorable. Some joined organized rallies, but most boats went on their own, as we did.

At the nearest point, the Canary archipelago of seven islands is located just fifty-four miles from the coast of Africa. We had a 450-mile crossing from Morocco to Lanzarote Island, our first landfall in the Canaries.

Motoring into Port Naos harbor just after dawn, it was wonderful to see over thirty cruising sailboats at anchor, many of whom we knew. Everyone was getting ready to cross "the pond".

We had allowed a month in the Canaries, and were uncertain as to which island had the facilities we needed. We had been saving up repair jobs for this period, and were delighted to give some of the work to other cruisers.

In Port Naos Anne, from the British boat, SKUNDA brought her heavy-duty sewing machine on board CORMORANT and stitched weak points in our mainsail. Gan, a Dutchman on AVENTURA, got our Autohelm and depth sounder working. Phil, our New Zealand friend on GOLDEN APPLE, helped Ward solve the engine oil leak that had plagued us since Singapore, and together they checked all the rigging.

The nearby town of Arricife offered what we needed in the way of banks, telephones, boat supply stores, supermarkets, and film developing. After a week of hard work, we rented a car for a day of sightseeing with Canadians Rene and Marlene on SARPEDON, a Corbin 39 like ours. We had met them in Tahiti three years before.

Lanzarote is a volcanic island as are all the Canaries, and much of it resembles a moonscape, especially around Fire Mountain in Timanfaya National Park. A series of volcanic eruptions in the early 1700's left vast lava fields and a row of craters, which cover much of the island. The last eruption, in 1824, left the gigantic crater of Fire Mountain.

We had to board special buses to ride along the rim and over the nearby blackened landscape, along precarious turns and past breathtaking drop offs. At a restaurant near the summit of the mountain, chickens were being roasted on a grill heated only by the smoldering volcano.

Throughout the island, where the landscape is blacker than the narrow road on which we traveled, little circular walls of lava had been built to create areas for growing grapevines in the rich volcanic soil. Artist and architect Cesar Manrique hailed from Lanzarote, and we enjoyed seeing his uniquely designed home which is now a museum housing much of his work, as well as original works by Picasso.

Our boat work finished, we sailed further west to the port city of Las Palmas, on the island of Gran Canaria. More than 160 sailboats preparing for the 1995 Atlantic Rally for Cruisers (ARC) were crowded into the marina, all festooned with signal flags, a spectacular sight.

Gran Canaria gave its name to the entire island group, but it is not the largest, as the name implies. Gran comes from Guanches, the original inhabitants. The name Canaria derives from *canis* the Latin word for dog; early discoverers of the island found huge dogs there. Canary birds, now found here in great numbers, take their name from the islands.

Another long day of sailing brought us to the island

of Tenerife, largest of the Canaries, and familiar to most of the world because of an airline disaster there several years ago. This was an important stop for us since we had mail waiting.

We tied to the city dock along with several other sailboats, right in the bustling heart of Santa Cruz, a large, cosmopolitan city. Stately government buildings and a handsome clock tower surround the nearby Plaza de Espagna, and well-groomed parks are scattered throughout this city of broad, shaded avenues.

Spain was the cleanest, most efficient of all the European countries we visited. In Santa Cruz, as in the rest of Spain, we found that cars stopped for pedestrians in crosswalks, and teams of uniformed street sweepers were at work early every morning.

Joanna and Lindsey Hackett, Australians from the sailboat ONAWA, joined us in renting a car for a day. We drove along the elevated spine of this lush, mountainous island to see Tenerife's most distinctive landmark, 12,000-foot high Mount Teide, fondly referred to as "El Pico" by the locals.

At one overlook along the forested road, we came upon a cluster of people enjoying a glass of wine. An elderly man was selling home brew out of a huge plastic jug, and his jovial wife was offering fresh-cooked apple turnovers out of the back of their dilapidated van. Needless to say, we indulged.

Closer to the mountain, forest gradually gave way to bare lava fields as the cone-shaped crater came into view. A cable car took us almost to the summit, where our thin jackets and shorts were poor protection from the cold blast of air. After hiking across a jagged lava path to the far side for a view of the sea, we shivered our way back to the lodge where hot chocolate hit the spot as we waited for the cable car to take us down.

We stopped in the ancient seaside village of Icod de los Vinos, to see a tree said to be over 1,000 years old.

Shops along the picturesque public square offered excellent local wines to taste and buy.

On another day we took a local bus to the rugged northwest side of the island, where the sea crashed upon jagged rocks far below. We continued on to a picture-perfect, man-made crescent beach on the quiet eastern side.

All the while in Tenerife we gradually stocked up on groceries at the modern supermarkets for our upcoming Atlantic crossing. We made many trips to the large, open air market, called Our Lady of Africa, for all the fresh fruits and vegetables the boat would hold.

Two days after our crew, Jack and Joyce Munsey from Annapolis arrived, we began our crossing. Our course out into the ocean took us right past the tiny island of Gomera, where in 1492 Columbus had filled his water kegs and made final provisioning before his historic voyage.

THE ATLANTIC CROSSING
(2,965 nautical miles in 29 days)

This would be the last ocean crossing of our circumnavigation and we wanted to do it right. From our study of the Atlantic Pilot Charts, we knew that the best time to cross from the Canary Islands to the Caribbean was between November and February. Planning for a three-week passage but provisioning for forty days, we decided to leave the Canaries in time to reach Barbados before Christmas.

About two dozen other boats were leaving around the same time, and most agreed to make radio contact twice a day during the crossing. While this was mainly for the comfort factor of knowing someone knew your location and status, it also proved a wonderful source of weather information as our group spread out over about 1,000 miles.

Following the traditional route first sailed by Columbus, we aimed south by southwest for the first 600 miles. We wanted this leg to be pleasant and smooth as Jack and Joyce reacquainted themselves with CORMORANT and its constant motion.

Large, confused seas with 25-knot winds on our stern quarter gave us rough, rolly conditions. The nights were just endured, and the only way to enjoy it was to sleep, fitfully. We were looking for the North Equatorial Current and trade winds that would allow us to turn west, putting the wind and seas behind us for the final 2,000 mile run to Barbados.

There is always good weather if you're patient, and by the fifth day we were barrelling along making over 140 miles a day in steady winds and seas. Though we were all tired from the erratic motion of the first few days, our routine was established, meals were being consumed, and even a book or two being read.

From boats ahead of us we learned three boats had broken their forestays, and REAL TIME had blown out her mainsail and was altering course for the Cape Verde Islands for repairs.

Twice the radio proved to be a life-saver as one of our group diverted 400 miles to tow a German sailboat in the ARC to safety after it lost its rudder. In another case several yachts hovered nearby as a French trimaran broke apart in rough seas. The crew of four adults and four children abandoned the boat and were taken aboard a passing freighter bound for New York.

In beautiful sunshine on our sixth day, just as we were feeling smug for having no damage from those rough and rolly conditions, a loud CRACK sounded throughout the boat. Jack, who was on the wheel, called below to Ward, "I have lost all steerage!"

A link on the steering chain had broken and the chain was laying uselessly in a pile in the engine room below. Fortunately, CORMORANT is equipped with a secondary (inside) steering system which uses hydraulics, not related to the chain and cable of the primary system.

While Judy steered from inside for three hours, Ward and Jack jury-rigged the chain. We were just 250 miles north of the Cape Verde Islands, so we decided to divert there to seek a more permanent fix to our broken chain.

Since we hadn't planned on going to the Verdes, we had only large scale charts on board. Using our radar, and with instructions on the radio from REAL TIME and ONAWA, who were already at anchor there, we were able to negotiate the last twenty miles among outlying islands. It was well after dark when we finally dropped anchor in Mindello harbor on the island of Sao Vicente.

Cape Verde is an independent country consisting of eight major islands scattered across 150 miles of ocean, lying 300 miles west of the bulge of Africa. They gained their independence from Portugal in the mid-1960's and are struggling economically. High unemployment and a rather bleak geography haven't dulled the spirit of the people, a pleasant mix of African and Portuguese.

In our brief sixty hours there we dinghied ashore and met Nilton Lopez, a seventeen year old "boat boy" who helped us find fuel, water, and supplies. We also found a motorcycle shop where our steering chain was repaired for $1.50.

We met KING DAVID, a North Sea sixty-foot wooden Trawler owned by Mike and Kirsten Hughes. With their two sons, eight month old Caleb and two year old Adam, they were headed from Denmark to the Falkland Islands to follow God's call to establish a mission for sailors there.

Back on the high seas, we sailed west in company with ONAWA. Within a day we had lost sight of each other and for the next 2,000 miles we saw only one other sailboat, such is the vastness of the Atlantic Ocean. The seas were still confused, and strong winds blew for three days. Two snowy white egrets, blown off their course, sought refuge on CORMORANT for twelve hours.

We fell into a windless hole, and for five agonizingly calm days budgeted our fuel and water. One morning we sat perfectly still on glassy seas, waiting for a breath of wind. Often we made less than seventy-five miles a day, most of that when our blue and white drifter (a light nylon sail) billowed in the light winds.

Once a group of pilot whales was right in our path. They had no interest in us as we drifted within twenty yards of them. We could swim and bathe in the calm waters and it was while swimming, tied to the stern by a long line, that Ward realized we had finally entered the North Equatorial Current. We were moving westward at about two knots, with no wind.

Good food prepared by Joyce and Judy sparked each day. The grinding routine of the watch schedule gave each of us time on the wheel and time off to read and sleep. We celebrated as we passed the halfway mark, about when the steady trade winds took effect. Christmas was observed at sea, as was Ward's birthday and a very special wedding anniversary for Jack and Joyce, as they renewed their vows thirty-eight years later.

The radio kept us aware of each boat's arrival in Barbados, and now, on a brisk wind, we seemed to roar along for our final 300 miles. Finally the dark shape of Barbados appeared under a white cloud on the horizon. Thirty-five miles later we rounded the island's southern tip and sailed along the beautiful coastline where we could see hotels, white beaches, and sailboards gliding by in the warm sunshine.

As we turned into the lee of the island and the security of Carlisle Bay, we anchored among forty other sailboats. It was like coming home! We had gone 2,965 nautical miles in twenty-nine days (including our two and a half days in Cape Verde); we had consumed two hundred gallons of water, ninety gallons of fuel, sustained no major damage to the boat, and had enough supplies to keep going. Finally our last ocean was behind us.

FESTIVE LANDS A WELCOME SIGHT
(We get hooked on Barbados' charm, Trinidad's Carnival)

Tropical sunsets framed by palm trees, blue waters, white sandy beaches and delicious rum punches offered an overwhelming welcome to weary sailors arriving in Barbados. After nearly a month at sea, we could not get enough.

Barbados is the easternmost of the Caribbean islands, and so far south that it is considered to be almost out of the path of hurricanes. However, an errant storm had recently wiped out the pier in Carlisle Bay, where we were anchored. Each trip ashore meant negotiating our dinghy through small, rolling waves. We would wear bathing suits, then change into our clothes at The Boathouse Restaurant. This friendly home-away-from-home for cruisers was located right on the beach. We received our mail there, did laundry, showered, and enjoyed many a congenial evening with fellow cruisers watching the sunset beyond the beachside palms.

Nearby Bridgetown, the capital of Barbados, was a flurry of cars, trucks, and tourists from visiting cruise ships. Mostly descended from former slaves, the Barbadians (or Bajans, as they call themselves) are jovial and friendly. It seemed that all the women wore hats, usually with a flower on the brim.

The rolling Barbados landscape looks a lot like the English countryside. From the mid-1600's, sumptuous English manor houses presided over scores of sugar plantations. Sugar was the main source of income in Barbados until tourism took over in recent years.

The stone walls of one plantation house remain, and it was there that the movie, *Island in the Sun*, with Harry Bellefonte, was filmed in the 1950's. From its spacious lawns the rugged Atlantic coastline lay far below. Named

Farley Hill, this site has been preserved as a National Park.

Riding a public bus, which seemed to go recklessly fast, we twisted along the ridge of the island. In the Barbados Wildlife Preserve we and our companions for the day, cruising friends from Australia and England, walked among deer, peacocks, iguanas, monkeys and giant turtles.

On the calmer west side, we stopped in Speights-town, a fishing village. At The Wharf Restaurant we had the island specialty for lunch: flying fish. Annie, our jolly, smiling waitress was wearing a hat, of course.

For many years Trudy Smyth has provided daily weather information to boats crossing the Atlantic, via Ham Radio from Barbados. One day she and her husband invited thirty of us to lunch at their home high on a cliff overlooking the sea. They must have thought we had not had enough rum punch back at the bay, and before the afternoon was over a few cruisers, ourselves not included, landed in their swimming pool, fully clothed.

Soon it was time for us to leave and head south for Trinidad, where CORMORANT would be hauled out for a general sprucing-up after nearly five hard years at sea. Labor there is known to be inexpensive and excellent.

During our overnight sail, speeding along and covering nearly 180 miles in about thirty hours, we caught a thirty-inch tuna, our first fish since the Pacific Ocean four years earlier. We had bought new hooks, lures, and lines in Barbados, after being the only boat that didn't catch a fish coming across the Atlantic. Now we had enough fish to feed twenty people!

* * * * *

The coast of Venezuela was in clear view as we rounded the northwest corner of Trinidad and entered

Chaguaramas Bay, to join dozens of yachts at anchor. There had been a U.S. Naval Base here from 1941 until the mid 1960's; now boat yards, built mostly in the last five years, lined the shore.

CORMORANT was hauled out and propped up at Power Boats boat yard. Within a few days we had arranged for a complete paint job on the sides and bottom, construction of a cockpit dodger and bimini, new sail covers and cockpit cushions, and sanding and refinishing of the interior floors. This work took four weeks to complete, and we lived on board during it all.

Trinidad, by far the largest of the Eastern Caribbean islands, prides itself in being "for every race and creed". Discovered by Columbus in 1498, its original inhabitants, the Caribs, gave way to emancipated slaves from Britain and a large number of East Indians, also brought in by the British. These two groups make up over eighty percent the population today. Dutch, French, Spanish and English all had their turn in governing Trinidad and its companion island, Tobago. In 1962 they combined to become the independent country of Trinidad and Tobago.

Tourism has not caught on here as much as in other Caribbean islands, even though the annual Carnival is known to be the finest in the West Indies. Calypso music and the steel band, or "pan", originated here and is heard year-round.

Though we did not stay for Carnival, which takes place the two days before Ash Wednesday, we experienced pre-Carnival activities. Neighborhood bands practice for weeks, perfecting their entries in the "pan" competition. Men, women, and children gather in open lots in the suburbs of the capital city, Port of Spain, their steel kettle-instruments mounted on moveable trailers, practicing for the big event. We could meander among them, our ears filled with that loud, pleasing metallic harmony.

Carnival is about masquerade too, called "mas" by

the locals. Craftsmen labor for weeks with sewing machines, knives, scissors, and glue-guns, constructing elaborate costumes, some as large as a two-story building, for the Grand Parade. Late one night we were shown into a "mas camp", as the workshops are called. We found an elderly man constructing huge papier mache Coca Cola bottles, on special order for the Olympics in Atlanta.

Our boat work nearly completed, we rented a car and drove across the island to the northeast corner, where the dense rain forest meets the sea. We enjoyed a quiet weekend away from the boat yard at beachside Mt. Plaisir Estate, a small wilderness resort. The Grande Riviere, originating high in the mountains, gushes down to form a fresh water lake right by the sea. Giant leatherback turtles swim ashore there between March and September to lay their eggs.

Saying good-bye to our boat yard friends and to Australian and New Zealand cruisers who were bound for Panama, we sailed north to Grenada.

JEWELS OF THE SEA—THE WINDWARD ISLANDS
(We loved being lagooned on these treasures)

To sail among these splendid islands is to revel in history, yet our knowledge of the Caribbean was skimpy at best. We had done some research, and now we would explore as many islands as we could, filling in the gaps of our understanding.

By most accounts, the Windward Islands are the six major islands and hundreds of smaller islets and cays that lie in an arc from Grenada northeast to Martinique. Bequia, St. Vincent, and St. Lucia lie in between, and on a clear day you can see from one island to the next. Barbados, also part of the Windwards, lies more than 100 miles to the east.

Much of the Windward Islands' history lies in their proximity to each other and their angle to the prevailing easterly winds. Columbus discovered them during his voyages to the New World. They were inhabited by the Arawak and later the Carib Indians. When the search for gold intensified in the 1600's and 1700's, island bases from which to interdict the flow of gold became quests in themselves. Portuguese, Spanish, English, French, and Dutch sailed these waters, fought over these islands, and colonized them.

Grenada gained independence from England in 1974. Nicknamed the Spice Island for its large nutmeg production, it is still struggling to be self-sufficient. Following the brief American military intervention in 1983, tourism now flourishes, with one or two cruise ships squeezing into the tiny harbor daily. The town of St. George's is quaint and picturesque, with narrow streets and busy market-places.

We went to the airfield where Army Rangers and elements of the 82nd Airborne Division landed in 1983.

Painted signs of support for the U.S.A. grace many a wall throughout the island, and people we met praised the American intervention.

Soon after we anchored in the well-protected lagoon of St. George's, we were joined by our son, Marcel, and his father-in-law, Gene Ferguson, both from Roanoke, Virginia. We also linked up with Joanna and Lindsey from ONAWA, whom we had last seen as we sailed west from the Cape Verde Islands two months before.

The six of us toured the island by van, visiting a nutmeg factory and the oldest rum distillery in the Caribbean. Mechanization hasn't grabbed hold here yet; most of the nutmeg processing and rum distilling is still done by primitive methods.

As ONAWA sailed south and west for Panama, we sailed north to the Grenadines, the most picturesque of all the Windward Islands. Among these hundreds of small islands are some of the whitest beaches and most azure waters in the Caribbean. In the Tobago Cays we anchored behind a half mile wide reef where we were totally protected from the swells of the Atlantic.

In Admiralty Bay on Bequia Island we anchored fifty yards from the shore. We had easy access to a walkway along the water's edge, lined with small hotels and quaint restaurants. Gene, a musician by profession, took over the keyboard at one spot to entertain us and the guests with his talent.

Since we were taking five years to sail around the world, it seems like we should have been able to stop at every island, but that's just not possible. St. Vincent was one of those we decided to pass. It had been a British possession for 200 years before its independence in 1979, and is now probably the poorest of the Windward Islands. We sailed close by its profuse, verdant coast, then crossed the rough twenty-mile ocean passage to St. Lucia, another former British possession set free in the 1970's.

We aimed for the Pitons, those distinct twin peaks that are the symbol of St. Lucia, easily visible from St. Vincent. Arriving at sunset, we soon realized it was far too deep to anchor where we had intended. A resort complex had established permanent moorings for rent, so we took the only one open.

An hour later we were asked to move when an 80-foot yacht appeared, claiming its reserved mooring. Now well after dark, we scrambled to find a spot at a pier, next to a 100-foot British yacht. We spent a very unpleasant night with CORMORANT yanking on her dock lines in surging waters.

There were some wonderful stops in St. Lucia: Marigot Bay, its flat, calm waters ringed with mangroves; Castries, the capital where cruise ships came and went 100 yards away; and Rodney Bay. There, inside the protected lagoon, it was an easy dinghy ride to popular Rodney Bay Marina.

After Marcel and Gene left us we waited for good weather, then scooted twenty-five miles northeast to the French island of Martinique. The last eight miles proved very difficult as we bashed into prevailing winds and seas nearing our destination.

*   *   *   *   *

France considers Martinique an integral province, or state, and as a result the economy there was boomng, compared to the newly independent island nations we had just left. The roads, airport, and capital of Fort de France were well maintained and resembled a tropical, affluent Paris.

Our son, Ward, and his wife, Debbie joined us in Cul de Sac du Marin, a charming anchorage on the southeast corner of the island. Sailing short distances downwind each day during their week-long stay with us, we enjoyed the water and shore life of the village of St. Anne, and the spectacular beaches of Les Anses de'Arlets.

During their last two days with us we anchored off the posh hotels of Anse Mitan and rented a car for a trip around this magnificent island. We stopped in the rain forest, walking to a waterfall where we waded in the natural pool below. On this dark and rainy day all the butterflies were in hiding when we stopped at the butterfly park.

We stood on the wild east coast where the Atlantic swells crashed ashore without mercy. At Trois Ilets, near our anchorage, we visited the home of Napoleon's Josephine, the Creole beauty who became Empress of France.

As we left Martinique, sailing downwind towards the Leeward Islands, Mount Pelee loomed above the receding shoreline. Pelee erupted in 1902 killing all but one of the residents of St. Pierre, then the capital of Martinque.

Aptly named, the Windward Islands were beautiful but we often had to beat into the wind as we headed north along the chain. We hope to return one day to visit those islands we missed.

SMOOTH SAILING IN THE LEEWARD ISLANDS
(Hurricanes take their toll; recovery is ongoing)

After the Windward Islands, the Leewards were a welcome change. A slight turn to the west gave us a smooth ride, with comfortable seas and the prevailing east wind aft of our beam. Alone during this stretch, we set out to sample the international flavor of yet another string of luxuriant, green islands.

Mountainous and verdant Dominica became an independent member of the British Commonwealth in 1978. It is off the beaten track for tourism. We moored in front of the rustic Anchorage Hotel in Roseau Bay, where the guests were a hardy group who had come to hike and enjoy the waterfalls, hot springs, and unusual flora. We regretfully sailed away the following morning, taking advantage of good wind and weather.

A group of French islands, the Iles des Saintes, near Guadeloupe, lay next in our path. As with Martinique, these islands are considered to be part of France, with well maintained roads, fine French cuisine (with a Caribbean flair), and a feeling of order and affluence.

The inhabitants of the Saintes are descended from French Bretons, and the lacy, carved trim on houses and gabled roofs, as well as typical round fishermen hats worn by some of the older men, reflect the look of Brittany, on the Atlantic coast of France.

Our anchorage in Terre Haut, largest of the Saintes, was filled with colorful wind surfers darting about, dodging the small ferries that arrived morning and night from Guadeloupe. High red cliffs rose from the turquoise waters. Perched on one hilltop overlooking the harbor was Fort Napoleon, our early-morning destination on a rented scooter.

Built in the 1800's and meticulously maintained, the

fort now houses a museum. Huge glass cases contain small ship models depicting the French-English Naval Battle of 1792. The better organized, better disciplined, and better equipped British forces soundly defeated the French in the very waters we had sailed across the day before.

On our scooter we easily covered the entire island, stopping for a picnic lunch on a shaded beach by the Bay of Pontpierre. A swim later near Sugarloaf Mountain, and a hike to a lookout on the other side of the harbor completed the day's outing.

*   *   *   *   *

Guadeloupe, the butterfly-shaped island, lies just to the north of the Saintes. Shallow draft boats can save eighty miles of the journey north to Antigua by going through the River Salee passage, which bisects Guadeloupe.

Once a day, in the pre-dawn darkness at precisely 5:00 a.m., the bridge opens, and waiting yachts glide silently through the narrow opening. Due to a time mix-up and a brief grounding of CORMORANT, we missed the opening one day and so were eager and ready when our turn came the following day.

We easily made it through the narrow opening, then anchored in the still waters just beyond the bridge to wait for daylight. There we watched as a huge flock of white egrets awakened and left their nests in the mangrove trees. We had witnessed their arrival in the glow of dusk the evening before. In the morning light we motored through the still waterway, a distance of about ten miles.

Approaching the final stretch, with channel buoys and open sea in view, we came upon a British sailboat aground. They had started out ahead of us and aimed for what looked like the center of the channel. For over an hour we labored to pull them off, and just as we got them free, we promptly hit bottom ourselves. They then helped free us and we were both off, following three more miles of channel buoys through a shallow, reef-filled bay. Perhaps next time we would go around Guadeloupe!

*　　*　　*　　*　　*

After forty miles of perfect, fast sailing conditions we reached the formerly British island of Antigua. English Harbor, where we anchored, is a perfect "S" shape, totally unseen from the sea. Admiral Nelson hid his large fleet here two hundred years ago. Historic buildings, a drydock, and huge pillars that supported a sail loft have been turned into the modern Nelson's Dockyard, offering all services for modern yachts.

High on a cliff across the harbor entrance is Shirley Heights, with ruins of Eighteenth Century fortifications and barracks. From there we had a majestic view of the harbor. Steel band music now drifts down on the anchorage from twice-weekly barbecues offered there.

Antigua is surrounded by reefs, giving an aquamarine color to the waters. We covered the whole island in one day by rental car, visiting St. Johns, the capital city, and along the way passing many palm-fringed white sand beaches and posh resorts. Formerly a sugar-producing island, its countryside is dotted with the remains of sugar mills.

Our next destination was St. Martin, a distance a little too far for one day. After a long 70-mile day, we anchored off the northwest coast of St. Barthelemy. Named after Columbus' brother, this quiet French island is a getaway for the wealthy. The bay we were in used to belong to the Rockefeller family.

In September of 1995 Hurricane Luis made a direct hit on the dual-nationality island of St. Maarten/St. Martin. As we made our approach we could see that the

Dutch capital of Phillipsburg has a temporary mooring for cruise ships, which continue to call at this popular duty-free port. Piers are slowly being restored. What we thought were blue roofs turned out to be blue tarps, covering dozens of homes whose roofs were stripped away in the hurricane.

Simpson Bay lagoon, a large, totally enclosed area entered from both sides through draw bridges, was still ringed with boats wrecked by Hurricane Luis, which hit with horrendous winds up to 225 mph. We anchored in the Dutch side of the lagoon, where most of the damage occurred.

Driving around the island we saw more restoration activity on the French side, especially in lovely Marigot, the capital. Many beachside resorts and restaurants on both sides were still closed or wiped away, but it was evident that life was slowly returning to all areas.

Just to the north of St. Martin is Anguilla, where we paid an important visit. Edward and Weber Taylor, friends from Fredericksburg, were waiting for us when we anchored in front of their pink and white house in Road Bay. We were warmly greeted by the Taylors and their house guests, Waldo and Joanne Beck and Dan and Emily Williamson, also of Fredericksburg.

There followed three delightful days of visiting and touring this beautiful island. Hurricane Luis hit here too, leaving boats washed ashore and buildings damaged. Tons of sand have since been returned to some of the resort beaches by dredging from the sea. Homes of residents were badly damaged and we heard many accounts of flooding, electrical outage, and uprooted trees that can never be replaced.

One sandy islet a mile off shore in front of the Taylors' home had been a popular tourist attraction. During the hurricane it was under water for several days and lost all but one of its many palm trees. The island reappeared a few days after the storm and the Government has since replanted dozens of palm trees there. Anquilla represents the best of the Leeward Islands in the friendly attitude of the people and their obvious desire to restore the entire island quickly after nature's destruction.

Marcel on the bow approaching the Pitons, St. Lucia

CROSSING OUR TRACK, BOUND FOR THE U.S.A.
(Family and friends join us for these last days at sea)

Dawn broke and the islands of the British Virgins slowly popped up on the horizon. Soon we negotiated Round Rock Passage between Fallen Jerusalem and Ginger Island, and entered Sir Francis Drake Channel. This was a significant moment for us, as we watched the GPS click off our ever-changing position. We waited for particular coordinates to appear, and at 8:45 a.m. it finally read 18 degrees, 25.5 minutes north latitude and 64 degrees, 27.5 minutes west longitude. We had crossed our outbound track of five years ago and were now circumnavigators!

Good friends John and Francine Stevens, Canadians from BARON ROUGE, and Fleming and Margaret Sanderson, Americans on board NOVA, joined us as we celebrated the event that night at Pusser's Restaurant on Liverick Bay of Virgin Gorda. Both those boats had been with us crossing the Atlantic, and BARON ROUGE would complete a ten-year circumnavigation in British Columbia.

*   *   *   *   *

A few days later we were joined by our daughter, Sally and her husband, Mark Barstow to sail the beautiful waters of the British Virgin Islands. We were surprised to see fewer sailboats there than five years ago; probably charterers were scared away by reports of damage from last year's hurricanes.

Often we had picturesque anchorages to ourselves as we spent a week sailing around Tortola, the main island. Our favorite was Monkey Point where we snorkeled as pelicans dive-bombed for their meal right amongst us.

*   *   *   *   *

After a brief visit to Puerto Rico where we provisioned at Roosevelt Roads, we set off for the three-day sail to the Turks and Caicos in company with BARON ROUGE. We had missed these islands on our way south five years before, and were anxious to explore them.

Fair winds turned foul during our passage, and we arrived in Cockburn Harbor exhausted after a very rough night at sea. Though we spent nine days in the Turks and Caicos, much of it was at anchor behind Six Hills Cay on the shallow banks in windy, rainy conditions. These islands are not yet on the main "tourist trail", but the reefs and offshore wrecks make it a haven for serious divers.

When the weather eased, we sailed overnight to Georgetown, capital of the Exumas in the Bahamas. At the Peace and Plenty Hotel we linked up with John and Sara Wells from California, all eager to join us for the third time during our voyage.

For the first week we island-hopped north along the Exumas to the northern tip of Eleuthera. In the tiny seafaring village of Spanish Wells, we met descendants of British Loyalists who had settled there after the American Revolution. They live in a rainbow of pastel-colored homes and support a major fishing industry. Their accent is a delightful brogue; a mix of British, Scottish, and Bahamian, and they are fiercely proud of their heritage. We enjoyed our two days at this rustic port where we could walk around the town in half an hour.

After a month of sailing with BARON ROUGE, we said goodbye at Spanish Wells. They headed for the east coast of Florida and we sailed north to the Abacos, the group of islands at the northern tip of the Bahama chain.

We spent another week here with John and Sara,

mainly at Great Guana Cay. This splendid, rustic island is only three hundred yards wide, with a sheltered anchorage on one side and a spectacular white sand beach inside a coral reef on the ocean side.

Soon after the Wells left, our ten year old grandson, James Kellogg arrived to spend six weeks on board COR-MORANT. Doc and Peggy Bahnsen rejoined us, and the five of us sailed to many of the cays that are easy trips from the main town of Marsh Harbor, snorkeling on spectacular reefs each day.

On Elbow Cay we visited the lighthouse at Hope-town; the popular landmark was undergoing a face-lift painting of its distinctive red and white stripes when we climbed it. At pristine Man-o-War Cay we had a reunion with a sailing friend, Nick Ellison on board LUSTY WIND. We had last seen him in Tahiti in 1992.

As we rounded close to Whale Cay to enter a tricky passage, our motor abruptly quit! We had been motor-sailing into 20-knot winds and four-foot seas. Now with only the sails, we were able to fall off the wind with just enough distance and depth to clear the islet as we retraced our path. Within thirty minutes Ward found and fixed the problem (a broken fan belt) and we resumed our trip through the Whale Cay Passage back to Marsh Harbor.

Now with only James as our crew, we set out alongside John and Cathy Miller on BLUE RUN to cross the Gulf Stream and reach the U.S.A. Five years before John had helped Ward install our wind steering gear which ever since we have called "John Miller". John liked our boat so much that he bought a Corbin 39 and installed a Hydrovane like ours.

These were some wonderful moments, with a ten year old "captured" by grandparents on a 39-foot boat. Fortunately the three-day crossing was mild, with only six hours of rough seas and strong winds right in the middle of the Stream.

As we approached the Florida-Georgia coastline on our last night at sea, we could pick up "talk" radio programs full of Presidential Election Year chatter. In the morning it was great to see a U.S. Navy ship on maneuvers, and dozens of shrimp boats, looking like huge preying mantises, dragging their nets along the shallow waters of the Continental shelf.

Soon we entered the St. Mary's River and dropped anchor behind Cumberland Island, Georgia, CORMORANT's first landing on the U.S. mainland in almost five years. It was a relief to have the oceans of the world behind us, and begin anticipating our return to Virginia in just six weeks.

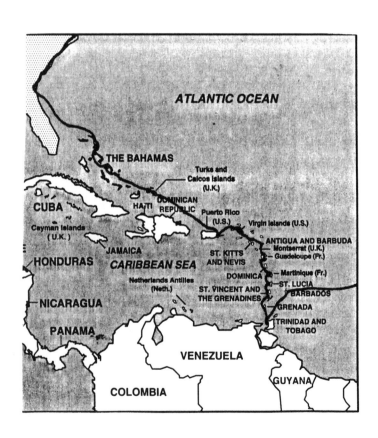

HOMEWARD BOUND DODGING A HURRICANE
(Safe in inland waters; Bertha finds us)

Retracing our steps of five years ago, we motored along Georgia's Intracoastal Waterway, exploring the barrier islands. Cumberland Island, a Carnegie family retreat in the early Twentieth Century, is a nature preserve reached only by boat. At lovely St. Simons Island we were greeted by our friend Lynell Stapleton, who gave us a quick tour of the island before we continued north.

In Savannah Ward's cousin, Luke Bowyer and his wife, Johnny met us at their dock. Five years before Johnny had lent us Sara, a pinafore-dressed teddy bear, to watch over us during our travels. We returned this world-traveler, now sporting a sarong and sunglasses, to Johnny's bear collection.

At Kiawah Island, South Carolina we caught our breath and enjoyed having our son, Marcel, his wife, Nancy, and their children, Barrett and Annie on board for a ride up Bohicket Creek to Rosebank Plantation. Huger Sinkler, our friend for the past twenty years, graciously offered us the use of his family's dock, as he had five years earlier.

Ten days later, Bill deCamp and his family, and Charlie and May Glenn joined us for the return trip to Bohicket Marina. There Durrant and Sara Kellogg, our teenaged grandchildren, replaced James as our crew before we continued north.

*   *   *   *   *

Following the red and green markers of the ICW past marshes and creeks, we were often accompanied by dolphins and watched by curious osprey, pelicans, and cormorants. We glided past Charleston's famous Battery,

281

and spent nights anchored in serene, though often hot and buggy, marshes. On the Fourth of July we anchored at the historic town of Georgetown, South Carolina, watching fireworks and the Parade of Boats, all patriotically decorated.

In Myrtle Beach we started tracking Hurricane Bertha as it first appeared in the Eastern Caribbean. After an evening in the home of Judy's aunt and uncle, John and Ginny Clevenger in Calabash, we enjoyed a vigorous ocean sail from the South Carolina/North Carolina border to Bald Head Island at Cape Fear. Another long day of motoring through the narrow Waterway brought us to an anchorage behind the protective peninsula of Wrightsville Beach, North Carolina.

By now Bertha was a mature hurricane, blasting the Caribbean islands we had recently sailed among (Turks and Caicos, and Abacos). It seemed like Bertha was following our exact path...looking for us! We decided to keep going north on the ICW, paralleling the shore, until we could turn inland at Morehead City to find shelter in a protected creek.

Falling in line with local boats of all sizes and shapes hurrying to take cover, we reached Cedar Creek, where other sailboats were already making preparations. We set three anchors, lashed our sails down, removed our bimini and dodger, and stowed all moveable items below. Just as we headed ashore to seek shelter, a local resident, Sue Mercer, motored out to the boats at anchor. She offered her waterfront home to any boaters who wanted to use it while she drove to her daughter's home further inland. Seven of us from three boats jumped at the opportunity.

From Sue's porch we watched anxiously as the winds built up, slacked off, then hit with a frightening sound. The eye had come ashore near Wrightsville Beach with 115 mph winds, and now its path would take it close by. Winds up to 85 mph slashed us for eight hours, spewing foam across the water and whipping through the trees, snapping off small branches.

When the power failed, we had to bucket water from the creek to flush the toilets. Telephones, a solace during a tense evening of tornado warnings, were dead the following morning.

After thirty-six hours we left Sue's house, which hadn't been hurt at all, and headed back to CORMORANT. It was a relief to find not a bit of damage and all systems on board working, even though three neighboring boats had washed up on the shore.

We thanked God for being spared, and sailed north on the Neuse River, headed for Virginia.

*   *   *   *   *

At Great Bridge, Virginia, tied to the wall of Atlantic Yacht Basin, we said good-bye to Durrant and Sara when our son, Ward, picked them up in late July. Now on our own for the remaining miles to Annapolis, Maryland, our "official" finish line, we enjoyed working hard on CORMORANT.

Ward replaced all the pilot house windows...a big job, and when he finished, there were no leaks! We had off-loaded a trunk-full of items with Ward, Jr. and could see CORMORANT getting lighter.

We crossed Hampton Roads, and spent a night at Fort Monroe Marina, visiting Bill and Bobbe Hartzog in their quarters there. A grand sail up the Chesapeake took us to the Rappahannock River, where Linda and Jauncey Sweet had asked us to rest and "regroup" at their rustic cottage on the Northern Neck of Virginia...our first homecoming! We unloaded more items while there; our boat's water-line was getting higher and higher.

A two-day sail up the Potomac River put us at Rick Johnson's home on Marlboro Point, near Fredericksburg, where he assembled a welcoming crowd of friends and neighbors. Even the Mayor of Fredericksburg attended! Two nights later we docked at the home of Joe and Anne Rowe near the Patuxent River for another nice break on our journey to Annapolis.

Finally our day to end this saga arrived. Promptly at 4:00 p.m. on August 17, 1996 we approached the United States Naval Academy, and slowly glided in to a pier reserved for CORMORANT at the Robert Crown Sailing Center. We had "dressed ship" with all our signal flags flying, and were astounded to see nearly two hundred friends and relatives on the dock. All who had sailed with us over the five-year adventure wore their CORMORANT crew member tee-shirts... a lot of them dotted the crowd! One relative, Hugues le Hardy, came all the way from Belgium for our arrival celebration.

Our six grandchildren scrambled on board for hugs, then, amidst champagne, toasts, tears and speeches we greeted family and friends. Classmates of ours from high school and college, and even a classmate of Ward's dad, Admiral Charles Buchanan, at age 92, were there to toast our return.

Stocking up in the Canary Islands

With Jack Munsey on board, we prepare to leave the Canaries

Joyce Munsey doing dishes — Mid-Atlantic

"On the hard" at Power Boats, Trinidad

DESCRIPTION of CORMORANT

MAKE: Corbin 39.

TYPE: Pilothouse, Cutter sailboat (fiberglass).

BUILT:Hull in 1983 by Corbin Les Bateaux, Napierville, Canada. Completed and launched in 1986 by Don Ney, Riverton, NJ.

LENGTH: 39' WIDTH: 12' 1" DRAFT: 5'6"

DISPLACEMENT: 24,000 pounds.

FUEL CAPACITY: 78 gallons.

ENGINE: BMW Marine, 50 HP.

CRUISING RANGE: 780 nautical miles when motoring.

WATER CAPACITY: 200 gallons.

GALLEY: 3-burner, propane stove/oven; refrigerator/freezer; microwave oven; storage space for 60 days of provisions.

NAVIGATION SYSTEMS: Global Positioning System (GPS); Radar; Autopilot; Wind steering vane.

COMMUNICATION SYSTEMS: Single side-band radio; VHF radio.

POWER: Four large batteries; a pole-mounted wind generator.

ANCHORS: Two 35 lb CQRs; one Fortress 37X.

SAILS: Seven sails (main, staysail, yankee, 130% genoa, storm jib, storm try-sail, and a light-air MPS gennaker).

GENERAL: CORMORANT has a steering wheel in the pilothouse as well as in the cockpit. A small washing machine, dryer, TV, stereo, electronic keyboard, wood-burning stove and central heat and air conditioning are built-in. The boat is ideal for a couple to live aboard, but there is sleeping space for eight.

AFTERWORD

During our five years we sailed 33,100 nautical miles, visited sixty-two countries or major island groups, and along the way more than seventy "crew members" joined us for brief periods.

The highlight of our journey was meeting so many fascinating people; both local inhabitants and fellow cruisers.

High on our list of places to revisit one day are: Cartagena (Columbia), the Solomon Islands, Australia, Malaysia, Israel, Spain, Trinidad, Dominica, and the Abacos (Bahama Islands).

Our two favorite spots were Suvarov Atoll (Cook Islands), an isolated dot on the ocean 500 miles west of Bora Bora, and Chesterfield Reef, 600 miles east of Australia in the Coral Sea. There, thousands of birds nest on the ground, turtles clamber ashore like small tanks and sharks graze just off the reef.

Having looked the world over, we can see that America is truly the greatest nation on earth. People, as exemplified by Sue Mercer, who offered usher home during Hurricane Bertha, are the reason. Americans have a spirit, a vitality, and an opportunity that sets us apart.

*   *   *   *   *

With CORMORANT back at her home, "D" Dock of Watergate Apartments on Back Creek in Annapolis, we reconnected with Bob Marr and Dave Boswell who first helped us tie up there over seven years ago. Eight months later we sold CORMORANT to Jane and Harry Hungate. They plan to sail her around the world again and we were thrilled to pass her on to them since we don't plan to cross any more oceans by sailboat.

We thank God for giving us the opportunity to fulfill this dream, and we thank our family and friends for their love, prayers and support which sustained us through all the challenges of this adventure.

*   *   *   *   *

Now we're seriously considering hiking the Appalachian Trail!

Homecoming — Annapolis, Maryland
August 17, 1996

ACKNOWLEDGEMENTS

We are indebted to hundreds of people who helped us on our journey. Among them, we especially thank:

Don and Becki Ney for building CORMORANT, our strong and sturdy boat.

The entire MARS "AFLOAT" Network of Ham Radio operators in the U.S.A. for always being there when we needed to talk. Fred Chapman, Tom Austin (who died soon after we reached the Red Sea), Warren Hogan, Bill Donaldson, Ken Hookansen, Vince Roebuck, and many other wonderful volunteers were essential to keeping our morale high.

Our fellow cruisers who gave so unselfishly of their time and talent to help us through some of our challenges. Among them are: New Zealanders Phil and Fay Atkinson, Tere' and Michael Batham, and Brian, Louise and Hedley Pearce; Australians Jack and Heather Williams, Rick and Lol Paynter, Bob and Toni Cruickshank, Lindsey and Joanna Hackett, and John Ivey; Canadians John and Francine Stevens; and Americans Richard and Kit Curtis, Sonia and Dixon Riley, Cathy and John Miller, and Sally and Andy Fleming.

Our crew, five of whom sailed with us on extended passages, and all of whom are mentioned in the book.

Linda and Jauncey Sweet, who helped us with our mail and emergencies, and our children

Sally, Ward and Marcel who managed our assets during our absence, and encouraged us throughout. Our Navy son, Peter, who had been an off-shore skipper with the USNA sailing team, was among the first to encourage us, saying, "You can do it!"

We also acknowledge those of the Free Lance-Star of Fredericksburg, VA who were so helpful in printing our articles over the five years:

Maria Carrillo, our editor, who was always up-beat, responsive, supportive and positive. Jennifer Sullivan and Scott Carmine who did the wonderful graphics that documented our trip, and Suzanne Carr, Robert Martin, and Norm Shafer who helped us with photographs. Special thanks to Jim Mann for his constant support.

Thanks also to Ron Magin, Automated Business Concepts in Fredericksburg, for expertly transforming our articles to "camera ready" form, and David Saunders, Book Crafters of Fredericksburg, for guiding us through the self-publishing world with efficiency and class.

TO ORDER ADDITIONAL COPIES OF THIS BOOK PLEASE SEND $11.95 (add 4.5% Sales Tax for books sent to Virginia addresses) TO:

ONCE AROUND
P. O. BOX 1907
FREDERICKSBURG,
VIRGINIA, 22402
(540) 371-6925
or
1-800-583-6590

INCLUDE SHIPPING AND HANDLING COSTS OF $2.00 FOR THE FIRST BOOK AND 75¢ FOR EACH ADDITIONAL BOOK SHIPPED TO THE SAME AD-DRESS.

INCLUDE THE NAME AND ADDRESS WHERE YOU WANT THE BOOKS SENT, AND ANY INSCRIPTION DESIRED.

(A 43-minute award winning video of CORMORANT's five-year voyage is also available. Price: $19.95. Tax, shipping and handling same as for book.)